Ex Líbrís

THE CIVIL WAR
QUIZ AND FACT BOOK

Also by Rod Gragg

Pirates, Planters and Patriots
Bobby Bagley: POW

THE CIVIL WAR QUIZ AND FACT BOOK

Rod Gragg

PROMONTORY PRESS

Published in 1993 by

Promontory Press
A division of Budget Book Service, Inc.
386 Park Avenue South
New York, NY 10016

Promontory Press is a registered trademark of Budget Book Service, Inc.

Published by arrangement with Harper Collins Publishers, Inc.

Library of Congress Catalog Card Number: 84-48162
ISBN: 0-88394-087-6

Printed in the United States of America.

For Cindy

CONTENTS

ACKNOWLEDGMENTS

One of the most enjoyable tasks of writing a book is thanking the people who contributed to it. I hope that the many people who assisted me in this work will recognize their contributions within its pages.

Several educators at the University of South Carolina's Coastal Carolina College provided professional assistance. Mary Bull, the public service librarian at Kimbel Library, cheerfully helped me track down peculiar facts and obscure information, and patiently responded to my repeated inquiries. Dr. Roy Talbert and Dr. Charles Joyner, historians at the college, offered advice and encouragement.

Ted Gragg generously conducted research for this book and made important suggestions about dates and naval actions. Professor George Adams of Montreat-Anderson College studied the manuscript with the critical eye of a Civil War expert and suggested several important changes. Steve Gragg also proofed the manuscript and offered suggestions.

M. S. Wyeth, Jr., executive editor at Harper & Row, kept me on deadline and made suggestions which improved my work. The staff of the Photographic Division of the Library of Congress provided valuable direction in selecting Civil War photographs. Other assistance came from the National Archives, the U.S. Army Military History Institute, the Horry County Memorial Library in Conway, South Carolina, and the Adams County Library in Gettysburg, Pennsylvania.

Others who provided assistance were Bill and Jackie Outlaw, David Parker, Bill Edmonds, Lisa Graham, Tommy and Kay Swaim, and George Taylor. My parents, L. W. and Elizabeth Gragg, helped in many ways. I am especially grateful for their encouragement.

One person whose assistance deserves a special expression of gratitude is Civil War authority Paul Fowler of Myrtle Beach, South Carolina. He contributed to this project from its beginning. His eye for detail and his broad knowledge of the subject added to this work immeasurably.

The most important contribution to *The Civil War Quiz and Fact Book* came from my wife Cindy, who proofed my writing, copied the manuscript, made valuable suggestions, endured my grouchiness at the deadline, and encouraged me to keep the perspective found in Matthew 6:33.

I am grateful to everyone who contributed to this work.

INTRODUCTION

No event in American history has attracted as many devoted students as the Civil War. It has commanded more attention, produced more books, and fueled more discussion than any other American war. More than a century has passed since the last arms were stacked and the final bugle was blown, yet there remains a phenomenal interest in the War Between the States.

Throughout the nation Civil War round-table groups assemble regularly to discuss, debate, or remember what happened at an obscure cornfield in Maryland, a rural peach orchard in Tennessee, or a muddy creek in northern Virginia. Publishers remain unable to exhaust the national appetite for new information about the conflict or even old information presented in a new manner. "Armies" in authentically detailed uniforms exchange mock gunfire in battle reenactments on old battlefields. Collectors amass treasured hordes of Civil War relics, literature, autographs, photographs, and artwork. Each year, despite the glittering lure of modern attractions, millions of Americans make pilgrimages to historic sites with nineteenth-century names like Shiloh, Chickamauga, Gettysburg, Kennesaw Mountain, and Antietam.

Why does a distant conflict continue to produce such fascination? Perhaps it is because the American Civil War was so unusual. It was the largest war ever waged on the North American continent. It was the first modern war and the last "romantic" war. It resulted in a remarkable number of wartime developments: the first battle between ironclad ships, the first national income tax, and the introduction of a host of inventions from instant coffee to aerial reconnaissance.

It was also an event of great human drama. In the flame of battle some men became instant heroes, while others who were already prominent saw their fame wilt. It was a war of great irony—brother fighting against brother, classmates pitted in combat against each other, crucial battles which could have gone either way. It produced acts of memorable courage, unpredictable cowardice, great marching armies, military foolishness and bungling, acts of genius, terrible brutality, and selfless sacrifice. After it ended, Americans could look back and clearly see it as a pivotal point in the nation's history—a war which ensured the unification of the nation under a strong national government.

It was also the first major war to occur in the presence of a modern communications industry. A pioneer corps of photographers recorded the men and events of the giant conflict while it raged; and when it was over, an industrialized printing industry produced an unprecedented barrage of personal narratives, regimental histories, military studies, and even a massive government-sponsored collection of key military records charting the warfare day by day.

This book is a unique contribution to Civil War literature: It is a collection of overlooked information, fascinating features, obscure details, and a few familiar facts, arranged in a format that will both intrigue the reader who knows little about the war and challenge even the most knowledgeable Civil War buff. It is an unusual book about an unusual event and is designed for the military historian in California, the relic collector in North Carolina, the Civil War buff in Kentucky, and the reenactment "soldier" in Pennsylvania—each a student of the American Civil War.

THE CIVIL WAR
QUIZ AND FACT BOOK

AMERICANS AT WAR

Q: How much money did the Civil War cost the U.S. government each day?

A: According to a report released by the U.S. Congress in 1863, the financial cost of fighting the war was $2.5 million a day.

Q: How many terms of office could the president of the Confederacy serve and how long was a term?

A: Confederate presidents were to be limited to one six-year term.

Q: Who was the owner of Ford's Theater, site of the Lincoln assassination, and what happened to him?

A: John T. Ford owned the theater, and after the assassination he was imprisoned for more than a month until the government admitted it had no evidence that he was a conspirator.

Q: Judged by population, what were the largest cities in the Union and the Confederacy?

A: According to the 1860 census, the Union's three largest cities were New York (805,651), Philadelphia (562,529), and Brooklyn (266,661); the Confederacy's three largest cities were New Orleans (168,675), Charleston, South Carolina (40,578), and Richmond (37,910).

(Library of Congress)

Q: When and where were Jefferson Davis and Abraham Lincoln first inaugurated?

A: Davis was inaugurated as provisional president of the Confederate States on February 18, 1861, on the steps of the Alabama capitol, left. Lincoln was inaugurated on March 4, 1861, on the portico of the U.S. Capitol in Washington, above.

Q: What were the "fireballs" used by Southern civilians?

A: When the South's supply of coal was exhausted, city dwellers mixed coal dust, sawdust, sand, and wet clay into hardened lumps called "fireballs," which they used to heat their homes.

Q: How many Federal and Confederate generals were West Point graduates?

A: Of the 583 generals in the Union army, 217 were West Point graduates; of the 425 Confederate generals, 146 had graduated from West Point.

Q: What *Northern* organization supplied thousands of products to *Confederate* soldiers during the war?

A: Despite wartime restrictions on communications and transportation, the Northern-based American Bible Society donated more than 100,000 New Testaments to Southern groups like the Confederate Bible Society, which then distributed the Scriptures to the Southern armies.

Q: What Civil War song was inspired by a telegram from Union General George B. McClellan?

A: The song "All Quiet Along the Potomac" was written as a poem by Ethelind Beers and was based on a dispatch from McClellan which reported a lack of enemy action near Washington.

Q: Which side suffered more battle deaths in the war, Union or Confederate?

A: Battle deaths were higher for the North, which recorded an estimated 110,000 killed or mortally wounded in battle, compared with an estimated 94,000 Confederate battle deaths.

Q: Who was Lincoln's first secretary of war and what happened to him?

A: Former Pennsylvania senator Simon Cameron served as the Lincoln administration's first secretary of war until he resigned on January 11, 1862, under accusations of corruption in the War Department. Two days after Cameron's resignation Lincoln nominated him to be minister to Russia and chose former attorney general Edwin M. Stanton as secretary of war.

Q: What financial bonanza befell the United States during the Civil War?

A: On May 26, 1863, gold was discovered in Alder Gulch, Montana Territory, providing a spectacular mineral harvest which reinforced the Federal treasury—already bolstered by California gold production.

Q: Who was chairman of the Joint Committee on the Conduct of the War, organized by the U.S. Congress to investigate controversial military actions?

A: U.S. Senator Benjamin F. Wade of Ohio was the chairman of the committee, itself controversial, which investigated selected military campaigns from Ball's Bluff to Fort Fisher.

Q: Who was the keynote speaker when the Gettysburg Address was delivered at the dedication of Gettysburg's national cemetery?

A: Noted orator Edward Everett of Massachusetts was the principal speaker; after Everett's two-hour oration, Lincoln delivered his brief Gettysburg Address.

Q: Why was New Hampshire balloonist Thaddeus S. Lowe arrested in South Carolina in 1861?

A: Soon to become famous for his military use of balloons with the Union armies, Lowe landed a balloon in South Carolina on a test flight from Ohio shortly after the fall of Fort Sumter and was temporarily arrested and imprisoned as a Yankee spy.

Q: How did Washington's Old Capitol Prison get its name?

A: Used to incarcerate Confederate prisoners and spies during the war, the Old Capitol Prison in Washington was originally built as a temporary capitol for the U.S. Congress after the British burned the U.S. Capitol during the War of 1812.

FACT: Confederate President Jefferson Davis and U.S. President Abraham Lincoln were both born in Kentucky—barely 100 miles apart and within eight months of each other.

Q: Who preached the sermon at Abraham Lincoln's funeral?

A: Dr. Phineas D. Gurley, pastor of Washington's New York Avenue Presbyterian Church, which Lincoln attended, delivered the sermon at the slain president's funeral.

Q: Where was the first capital of the Confederacy?

A: Montgomery, Alabama, was the first capital of the Confederacy and held that distinction from February 1861 until the following May, when the capital was moved to Richmond.

Q: Identify the following: "Johnny Fill Up the Bowl," "Just Before the Battle, Mother," "Lorena," "Tenting on the Old Campground," "Weeping Sad and Lonely," "The Homespun Dress," "Shoo Fly Shoo," and "Pop Goes the Weasel."

A: All were songs popular with Civil War soldiers.

Q: In the official exchange of prisoners, how many enlisted men were to be traded for a general?

A: According to official arrangements devised by Union and Confederate authorities, one general was worth 60 enlisted men, but a lieutenant was worth only four.

Q: What was the most common prewar profession for Confederate generals?

A: The largest number of Confederate generals were lawyers or judges before the war, followed closely by professional soldiers.

Q: Civil War zouave units patterned their uniforms after what foreign army?

A: Confederate and Union zouaves modeled their uniforms after North Africa's French colonial army, known for its baggy trousers, brilliantly colored uniforms, and distinctive fezzes and turbans.

FACT: The Medal of Honor, the highest decoration awarded members of the U.S. military, was created by the U.S. Congress in December 1861 as an award for Union naval enlisted men only; not until July 1862 were army troops authorized to receive the medal.

Q: What happened to Rose Greenhow, Washington's famous Confederate spy?

A: After her release from a Washington prison, Greenhow went to Europe; upon her return to the South, she drowned when her ship ran aground off Fort Fisher, near Wilmington, North Carolina.

Q: Who was postmaster general of the Confederacy?

A: John H. Reagan, a former U.S. congressman from Texas, was appointed Confederate postmaster general in March 1861 and held the post until April 1865, when he took the post of Treasury secretary for the final weeks of the Confederate government.

(Library of Congress)

Q: What was the official name of Andersonville, the notorious Confederate prison camp located in south Georgia?

A: Andersonville, above, which claimed the lives of more than 13,000 Union prisoners of war, existed from February 1864 until April 1865 and was officially named Camp Sumter.

Q: Who designed the Stars and Bars, the first official Confederate flag?

A: Composed of two wide red bars separated by a wide white bar, with seven white stars on a field of blue in the upper left corner, the Stars and Bars was designed by Southern educator Nicola Marschall early in 1861; it was officially put into Confederate service when it was raised over the Confederate capitol in Montgomery, Alabama, on March 4, 1861.

Q: What was the "official" name of the American Civil War?

A: Although known by such diverse names as "The War for Southern Independence," "The Brothers' War," "The Late Unpleasantness," and "The War of Northern Aggression," the conflict's most common name is "The Civil War." Generations of Southerners preferred "The War Between the States." But when the U.S. government published the massive *Official Records of the Union and Confederate Armies* in the late nineteenth century, the official name used for the conflict was "War of the Rebellion."

Q: Where did Julia Ward Howe write "The Battle Hymn of the Republic"?

A: She penned the famous Civil War song while a guest at Willard's Hotel during a visit to Washington.

Q: Who were the six men who held the post of Confederate secretary of war?

A: LeRoy P. Walker was the first, followed by Judah P. Benjamin, George W. Randolph, Gustavus W. Smith, James A. Seddon, and John C. Breckinridge.

Q: Who was the judge in the Lincoln assassination conspiracy trial?

A: U.S. Judge Advocate General Joseph Holt of Kentucky, a former cabinet member in the Buchanan administration, presided over the trial of the assassination conspirators and handed down the sentences to those condemned to death.

Q: What Northern state issued the first call for black troops in the Civil War?

A: Rhode Island.

Q: During the Civil War, more than 800,000 immigrants entered the United States. From which countries did the majority of the immigrants come?

A: The largest number of immigrants, 233,052, came from Germany, followed by 196,359 from Ireland and 85,116 from England.

Q: Who was George F. Root?

A: Root was a prolific Northern songwriter who composed a string of Civil War songs popular with Union soldiers, including "The Battle Cry of Freedom," "Tramp, Tramp, Tramp," and "Just Before the Battle, Mother."

Q: At war's end, how large was the national debt incurred by the Confederate government?

A: Two billion dollars.

Q: What was "ginger beer," consumed by Southerners when the war made "spiritous liquors" unavailable?

A: It was a mixture of molasses, ginger, water, and yeast warmed to fermentation.

Q: What cabinet post did Abraham Lincoln's son Robert hold after the war?

A: He became secretary of war in the Garfield administration.

Q: As a secret negotiator for the Confederate government, Congressman Duncan Kenner of Louisiana offered the British and French governments a concession in exchange for diplomatic recognition of the Confederacy. What did he offer?

A: Emancipation of Southern slaves.

FACT: The biggest killer in the American Civil War was not combat but disease. Of the estimated 623,026 soldiers who died in the war, an estimated 388,580—62 percent—died of disease. The leading cause of death on both sides was diarrhea, followed by typhoid, typhus and malarial fevers, pneumonia, smallpox, and measles.

Q: What were the Ironclad, Fort Sumter, Headquarters U.S.A., and the Blue Goose?

A: All were notorious Washington, D.C., bordellos operating during the Civil War.

Q: What official held three different cabinet posts in the Confederate government?

A: New Orleans attorney Judah P. Benjamin served the Confederacy as attorney general, secretary of war, and secretary of state.

Q: What percentage of the soldier vote did Abraham Lincoln win in his 1864 presidential campaign against General George B. McClellan?

A: Lincoln won 55 percent of the popular vote, including 78 percent of the tabulated soldier vote.

Q: What technological development did the Civil War bring to the American shoe-manufacturing industry?

A: The unprecedented demand for footwear for Union troops caused a shift from small shop production of shoes by hand to mass shoe production by factories equipped with leather-stitching machinery.

Q: What was the Gillmore Medal of Honor?

A: It was a medal developed by Union General Quincy A. Gillmore and awarded to Federal troops who had served with distinction in action against Charleston in 1863.

Q: What was the occupation of William Mumford, the New Orleans resident who was hanged by Union General Benjamin F. Butler for hauling down the American flag in occupied New Orleans?

A: He was a professional gambler.

FACT: When Union General Philip Kearny was killed in action during the war, his family barred members of the press from his funeral. However, *New York Times* reporter Joseph Howard got the story by attending the funeral disguised as a priest.

Q: Name the eleven Confederate states in the order in which they seceded.

A: South Carolina, Mississippi, Florida, Alabama, Georgia, Louisiana, Texas, Virginia, Arkansas, North Carolina, and Tennessee.

Q: Where did President-elect Abraham Lincoln stay in Washington before moving into the White House in 1861?

A: For 10 days prior to his 1861 inauguration, Lincoln stayed in Parlor 6 of Willard's Hotel.

(Library of Congress)

Q: How were newspapers circulated among Federal troops in the field and how much did they cost?

A: Most major daily newspapers, especially the powerful New York City papers, and many hometown weeklies mailed newspapers to Union soldiers for subscriptions. Some newspapers, however, were sold to the troops by sutlers or newspaper vendors like these. Although competition forced the price down occasionally, most newspapers were sold to soldiers for 10 cents a copy—an inflated price which caused the troops to chip in and pass around a shared paper.

Q: What coordinated action was taken by U.S. marshals throughout the North on Monday, May 20, 1861?

A: In an effort to uncover Confederate sympathizers and agents, U.S. marshals entered telegraph offices across the North and seized telegrams sent during the past year.

Q: What famous American author served as a nurse in a Union hospital during the war and later wrote a book about her experiences?

A: Louisa May Alcott, author of the classic *Little Women*, wrote *Hospital Sketches* in 1863, detailing her duties as a Civil War nurse.

Q: Where did Jefferson Davis last preside over the Confederate cabinet?

A: On April 26, 1865, while they were retreating south after the fall of Richmond, Davis presided over his cabinet for the last time while passing through Charlotte, North Carolina.

Q: What was Ulysses S. Grant doing when the war began?

A: Following a succession of professional failures, he was living in Galena, Illinois, where he was a clerk in a leather-goods store owned by his father and managed by his younger brother Orvil. Three years later he would be general-in-chief of the United States Army and seven years later would be elected president of the United States.

Q: What high-ranking Confederate official was imprisoned by the U.S. government for more than two years after the war ended?

A: Confederate President Jefferson Davis.

Q: Why did the crowd attending Abraham Lincoln's second inauguration have difficulty understanding the inaugural speech delivered by Vice-President Andrew Johnson?

A: Johnson had been prescribed whiskey by a physician as treatment of a minor medical condition. Prior to the inauguration Johnson exceeded the dosage, which rendered him somewhat intoxicated and caused him to deliver a rambling and sometimes incoherent inaugural speech.

Q: What two new states were admitted to the Union on June 20, 1863, and on October 31, 1864?

A: West Virginia, a new state formed by mountain Unionists in Virginia, was admitted first, followed the next year by mineral-rich Nevada.

Q: The mortality rate for Union soldiers in Confederate prison camps was approximately 15 percent. What was the mortality rate for Confederate troops in Northern prisons?

A: Of the 194,000 Federal troops in Southern prison camps, approximately 30,000 did not survive. Of the 214,000 Confederates imprisoned in the North, approximately 26,000—12 percent—died in captivity.

Q: Who was Abraham Lincoln's first vice-president and where was he from?

A: Senator Hannibal Hamlin of Maine was Lincoln's first vice-president. He was dropped in 1864 in favor of longtime Democrat Andrew Johnson of Tennessee.

Q: What facial decoration was temporarily in style during the Civil War and came to characterize the officers of both sides?

A: The beard.

Q: What was the population of the United States on the eve of the war?

A: According to the 1860 census, the population of the United States was 31,443,321. States which would remain in the Union had a total population of 22,339,989; states which would form the Confederacy had a total population of 9,103,332, including 3,521,110 slaves.

FACT: Of all the soldiers who served in the Union army during the Civil War, the largest age group—almost 40 percent—was composed of young men who were twenty-one years old or younger.

Q: When the Civil War began, what job was held by Clara Barton, above, the Civil War humanitarian who was instrumental in the creation of the American Red Cross?

A: She was a clerk in the U.S. Patent Office in Washington.

Q: Who wrote *Our American Cousin*, the play presented at Ford's Theater the night Abraham Lincoln was assassinated, and who played the lead in the production?

A: Playwright Tom Taylor was the creator of *Our American Cousin*, which starred actress Laura Keene.

Q: Who was William Jones and what was his relationship to Ulysses S. Grant?

A: Jones was a slave owned by Grant in the late 1850s, when Grant tried unsuccessfully to earn his fortune as a farmer. Grant later gave Jones his freedom, rejecting an opportunity to sell him for much-needed cash.

Q: Who was "Dragon Dix"?

A: Dorothea Dix, the superintendent of female nurses for the U.S. government during the war, was so described by some aspiring nursing applicants because she insisted that army nurses be at least thirty years old and "plain in appearance."

Q: What was Point Lookout?

A: Located at the junction of the Potomac River and Chesapeake Bay in Maryland, Point Lookout was a Federal prison camp for 20,000 Confederates during the last two years of the Civil War.

Q: For whom did Abraham Lincoln arrange a wedding ceremony before a joint session of Congress?

A: Nationally acclaimed for her humanitarian efforts and fund-raising on behalf of Union soldiers, Elida Rumsey was married to John Fowle before a special joint session of Congress and a capacity crowd of visitors in 1862—at the invitation of President Abraham Lincoln.

Q: How many Confederate and Union generals were killed or mortally wounded in action during the Civil War?

A: Seventy-seven Confederate generals and 47 Union generals were killed or mortally wounded in action, meaning that 18 percent of Confederate generals and 8 percent of Union generals died from battle wounds.

Q: What was the cost of a barrel of flour in Richmond in January 1864?

A: Two hundred and fifty dollars.

Q: In July 1863, a mob of 50,000 people set fires and looted buildings in New York City for four days, until it was dispersed by Union veterans of Gettysburg. What was the mob protesting?

A: On July 13-16, 1863, rioters objecting to the Federal military draft went on a destructive rampage in New York City, where they destroyed a black church, an orphanage, and several homes and offices, and caused more than a million dollars in damages before they were suppressed by Federal troops.

Q: What two members of the Lincoln administration observed Lincoln throughout the war while planning to publish a book about his presidency?

A: In 1861, shortly after Lincoln was elected, his private secretary, John Nicolay, and his assistant private secretary, John Hay, began gathering material about Lincoln for a jointly written biography, which was finally published in ten volumes under the title *Abraham Lincoln: A History*.

Q: How many men served in the Union and Confederate military?

A: An estimated 1.5 million to 2.2 million men enlisted in the U.S. forces during the war, compared to an estimated 600,000 to 1.4 million in Confederate service.

Q: What American tradition was established by the U.S. government on Friday, April 22, 1864?

A: Under an act of Congress the motto "In God We Trust" was first stamped on U.S. coins.

FACT: An estimated 3,200 women served as nurses in the Union army during the Civil War, while a somewhat smaller, undetermined number of women served as nurses for the Confederate forces.

Q: What were the primary occupations of Union and Confederate soldiers prior to the war?

A: According to a U.S. Sanitary Commission survey, 47 percent of all Union soldiers were farmers or farm workers and 25 percent were skilled laborers. A study of Confederate records indicated that an estimated 61 percent of all Confederate soldiers were planters or farmers, and 14 percent were skilled laborers.

Q: What was Ulysses S. Grant's given name?

A: Although best known today as Ulysses Simpson Grant, his name at birth was Hiram Ulysses Grant. At West Point, a clerical error officially listed him as Ulysses Simpson Grant, mistakenly replacing "Hiram" with his mother's maiden name, Simpson, which gave Grant the famous initials "U.S."

Q: Who was U.S. minister to Great Britain during the war?

A: The American minister to England, who did much to block British diplomatic recognition of the Confederacy, was former U.S. congressman Charles Francis Adams, who was the son of President John Quincy Adams.

Q: What Northern city was struck by Confederate sabotage on Friday, November 25, 1864?

A: On this date Confederate conspirators set coordinated fires in a dozen New York City buildings but did no serious damage.

Q: Which enacted the first military draft in American history—the Federal government or the Confederate government?

A: On April 16, 1862, Confederate President Jefferson Davis approved a conscription act passed by the Confederate Congress, and on March 3, 1863, almost a year later, President Abraham Lincoln signed into law a military draft act passed by the U.S. Congress.

Q: What was the difference between the Army of Tennessee and the Army of the Tennessee?

A: Both were Civil War armies. The Army of Tennessee was Confederate and was named for the state, while the Army of the Tennessee was Federal and was named for the Tennessee River.

Q: What was the inflation rate of Confederate money by the end of the war?
A: Approximately 9,000 percent.

Q: How old was John Wilkes Booth when he assassinated Abraham Lincoln?
A: Twenty-six.

Q: How many U.S. servicemen received the Medal of Honor for acts of bravery in the Civil War?
A: Approximately 1,200.

Q: What were "bounty jumpers"?
A: They were Union soldiers who joined the army to get the government's enlistment bonus, or bounty, then deserted to enlist again somewhere else, where they could claim another bounty.

Q: What was the largest railroad in the world at the time of the Civil War?
A: Created by the U.S. War Department in 1862 to provide supply lines for the Union armies, the U.S. Military Railroads improved captured Southern rail lines and built new ones, becoming the world's largest railroad in 1865—with 2,105 miles of track, 419 locomotives, and 6,330 cars.

Q: When wartime shortages depleted foodstuffs in the South, what did Southerners substitute for cream in their coffee and tea?
A: Egg whites and butter.

Q: What was Pfaff's Cave?
A: Located at 653 Broadway in New York City, Pfaff's Cave was a favorite bar and rendezvous for the Civil War correspondents of New York's press corps.

Q: What national holiday was established by President Lincoln during the Civil War?
A: On October 20, 1864, Lincoln proclaimed the last Thursday in November Thanksgiving Day, a national holiday, to commemorate "a day of Thanksgiving and Praise to our beneficent Father who dwelleth in the Heavens."

(Library of Congress)

Q: Who shot Lincoln assassin John Wilkes Booth?

A: Sergeant Boston Corbett, left, a cavalryman in the detachment of troops who cornered Booth in a Virginia tobacco barn, claimed to have fired the shot which mortally wounded Booth. Posed with Corbett in this photograph is one of the officers who participated in the hunt, Lieutenant E. P. Doherty.

Q: What were "artificial oysters"?

A: In an attempt to cope with the deprivations of war, Southern homemakers served meals of "artificial oysters"—grated green corn mixed with egg and butter, rolled in batter, and pan-fried.

Q: Who was General George B. McClellan's running mate in his race against Lincoln for the White House in 1864?

A: Lincoln and running mate Andrew Johnson of Tennessee were opposed by Democrat McClellan and his party's vice-presidential nominee, George H. Pendleton of Ohio.

Q: Which Federal prison camp held more Confederate prisoners during the war, Camp Douglas or Elmira?

A: Camp Douglas, located near Chicago and noted for its bitterly cold winters, was used to imprison more than 30,000 Confederate troops during the war. Elmira, established near Elmira, New York, in 1864, held approximately 10,000 captured Confederates during the war's last year.

Q: How did the Union army's demand for uniforms affect the U.S. clothing industry?

A: The number of sewing machines used by the U.S. garment industry doubled between 1860 and 1865, and manufacturers adopted a standardization of sizes for uniforms and civilian clothing.

Q: What was Jefferson Davis doing when he received the news that he had been chosen president of the Confederate States?

A: When the news arrived at Davis' Brierfield plantation near Vicksburg on Sunday, February 10, 1861, the president-elect was helping his wife Varina prune rosebushes.

FACT: Following the assassination of President Lincoln, the U.S. government seized Ford's Theater in Washington and later converted it into a government office building. Theater owner John T. Ford was eventually awarded $100,000 from the government as compensation for the confiscation of his property.

2 | CAMPAIGNS AND BATTLES

Q: Who was the Union soldier who found Robert E. Lee's famous "Lost Order" during the Antietam Campaign?

A: On September 13, 1862, as the Union Army of the Potomac entered Frederick, Maryland, one day behind Lee's Army of Northern Virginia, a copy of Lee's Special Order No. 191, detailing the Confederate invasion plans, was found wrapped around three cigars by Private B. W. Mitchell of Company F, 27th Indiana Volunteers. The copy was transmitted up the chain of command to General George B. McClellan, who used the information to bring Lee's army to battle at Antietam, ending Lee's 1862 invasion of Maryland.

Q: Fraley's Field, Bloody Pond, the Peach Orchard, Hell's Hollow, and the Hornets' Nest were landmarks of what major Civil War battle?

A: Shiloh.

Q: What was Ulysses S. Grant's first Civil War battle?

A: Grant's first Civil War engagement was the Battle of Belmont, fought on November 7, 1861. Grant, a brigadier general, captured a fortified Confederate position at Belmont, Missouri, overlooking the Mississippi River, but was later forced to retreat.

(Library of Congress)

Q: Was Fort Sumter ever retaken by U.S. forces during the war?

A: No. After the fort was occupied by Confederate forces in April 1861, it was not surrendered. However, it was evacuated at war's end by the retreating Confederate forces in Charleston and was repossessed by Federal troops in February 1865. Above, a lone Confederate cannon guards the fort's battered wall.

Q: What Civil War military campaign in 1864 was prompted by Napoleon's nephew?

A: Concerned about French Emperor Napoleon III establishing a puppet government in Mexico, Lincoln ordered the Union occupation of eastern Texas in 1864, which resulted in the controversial Red River Campaign.

Q: What well-known Confederate general was killed in action on June 14, 1864, at Pine Mountain, Georgia?

A: Confederate General Leonidas Polk, a corps commander under Joseph E. Johnston in the Army of Tennessee, was killed on this date by Federal artillery fire while holding a war council with other officers atop Pine Mountain, north of Atlanta.

Q: How many miles were covered by the Union cavalry during Grierson's Raid and how long did it take them?

A: On April 17, 1863, Colonel Benjamin H. Grierson and 1,700 Federal horsemen left La Grange, Tennessee, on a raid across Mississippi and Louisiana which ended on May 2—600 miles and 16 days later.

Q: Where was the longest pontoon bridge of the war and how long was it?

A: Erected across the James River during the Petersburg Campaign in 1864, the James River Bridge was the war's longest pontoon structure. It was 2,200 feet long, used 101 pontoons, and required 450 Union engineers for its construction.

FACT: The first serious land action of the war occurred on June 10, 1861, at Big Bethel, Virginia. Seven regiments of Federal troops numbering about 2,500 men left nearby Fort Monroe and marched toward Richmond until they encountered a well-fortified Confederate position manned by approximately 1,200 troops. After a brisk exchange of fire the Union forces were repulsed with a loss of 18 dead, while the Confederates recorded one combat death.

Q: The Battles of Mechanicsville, Gaines' Mill, Savage's Station, and Malvern Hill were fought in what 1862 campaign?

A: Called the Seven Days' Battles, they ended the Peninsula Campaign, in which Union General George B. McClellan tried to capture Richmond by an advance from the east.

Q: What 1862 campaign was fought around these landmarks: Ellerson's Mill, Beaver Dam Creek, Boatswain's Swamp, the Richmond-York River Railroad, and the Chickahominy River?

A: The Seven Days' Battles.

Q: What was the "Sickles Salient" at Gettysburg?

A: When the Union line moved into position on the second day of the Battle of Gettysburg, Union General Daniel E. Sickles, assigned the defense of the Federal left flank, moved his corps forward without orders to high ground over the Emmitsburg Road, forming what became known as the "Sickles Salient," including the hotly contested Peach Orchard, Wheatfield, and Devil's Den.

Q: Which side suffered higher casualties in the Confederate victory at Chickamauga?

A: The Confederates sustained the worst casualties: 18,454 losses, compared to Federal casualties of 16,170.

Q: After Union General Nathaniel Lyon was killed at the Battle of Wilson's Creek, who took command of the Federal forces for the rest of the battle?

A: Upon Lyon's death, Major Samuel D. Sturgis assumed command and ordered a withdrawal—an order which produced criticism but did not prevent Sturgis from receiving a promotion to brigadier general.

Q: How were battles named during the Civil War?

A: With some exceptions, Federal forces tended to name battles for the nearest body of water, while the Confederates usually named battles after the nearest community—practices which gave some Civil War battles more than one name, like Bull Run/Manassas and Antietam/Sharpsburg.

Q: What was the largest battle of the 1865 Carolinas Campaign?
A: On March 19–21, 1865, some 16,000 troops of Sherman's army under General Henry W. Slocum fought a fierce but inconclusive battle with a slightly larger force of Confederates under General Joseph E. Johnston at Bentonville, North Carolina—the largest battle of the Carolinas Campaign.

Q: What series of battles prompted this observation from Union General George G. Meade: "Grant has had his eyes opened and is willing to admit now that Virginia and Lee's army are not Tennessee and Bragg's army"?
A: Meade's observation followed the Battles of the Wilderness, Spotsylvania, and Cold Harbor in May and June 1864, when the Army of the Potomac under Grant suffered more than 43,000 casualties in action against Robert E. Lee's Army of Northern Virginia.

Q: Where did the bloodiest eight minutes of the war occur?
A: Grant's massive frontal assault against Lee's entrenched line at the Battle of Cold Harbor on June 3, 1864, resulted in approximately 7,000 Union casualties and 1,500 Confederate casualties within eight minutes—the bloodiest eight minutes of the Civil War.

Q: What Union victory, won on March 8, 1862, was the largest Civil War battle west of the Mississippi River?
A: The Battle of Pea Ridge.

Q: "It was not war—it was murder" referred to what battle?
A: Confederate General D. H. Hill used this phrase to describe the Battle of Malvern Hill, which produced 5,355 casualties on July 1, 1862.

FACT: The American Civil War consisted of more than 10,000 military actions, ranging from major military campaigns to minor exchanges.

Q: The Battles of Peachtree Creek, Ezra Church, and Jonesborough were actions in the 1864 Union campaign to capture what important Southern city?

A: They were part of the campaign for Atlanta, which fell on September 2, 1864.

Q: In what battle was the famous frontiersman "Kit" Carson cited for bravery?

A: Christopher "Kit" Carson, who would become famous as an Indian fighter, was a colonel of U.S. Volunteers in the New Mexico and Arizona campaign of 1861–62, in which he was brevetted brigadier general for his actions in the Battle of Valverde, New Mexico, on February 21, 1862.

(Library of Congress)

Q: For whom was Gettysburg named, how old was the town at the time of the battle, and what was its population?

A: Site of the war's biggest battle, Gettysburg, above, was named for Pennsylvania settler James Gettys, was 57 years old at the time of the battle, and had a population of approximately 2,400.

Q: From whom did General Ulysses S. Grant demand "unconditional and immediate surrender" in the message which made him famous as the victor of Fort Donelson?

A: Grant's famous declaration of terms was made to Confederate General Simon Bolivar Buckner, a prewar army friend of Grant's, who was left to surrender Fort Donelson when his superiors, General John B. Floyd and General Gideon J. Pillow, relinquished command to Buckner and escaped.

Q: At what battle was Confederate General "Stonewall" Jackson mortally wounded?

A: Jackson died of complications from a wound received when he was accidentally shot by his own troops at the Battle of Chancellorsville on May 2, 1863.

Q: Which Confederate charge was made over a longer distance—Pickett's Charge at Gettysburg or the charge by the Confederate Army of Tennessee at the Battle of Franklin?

A: At Gettysburg, Robert E. Lee's troops charged across an open field one mile long against makeshift Federal works, supported by a massive pre-assault artillery bombardment. At Franklin, Hood's Confederates charged across a *two*-mile-long open field against a heavily fortified Union position, unsupported by a heavy artillery barrage.

Q: What was the "Mud March"?

A: It was an unsuccessful attempt by Union General Ambrose E. Burnside to move the Army of the Potomac against the Army of Northern Virginia following the disastrous Federal loss at Fredricksburg in December 1862. A severe winter rainstorm turned Burnside's campaign into a "mud march," and it failed.

FACT: Black troops were first used in battle in the Civil War on October 29, 1862, when the 79th U.S. Colored Infantry engaged Confederate forces at the Battle of Island Mount in Missouri.

Q: The Battles of Cedar Mountain, Groveton, and Chantilly were part of what campaign?

A: Second Manassas.

Q: What was the largest battle ever fought in the Western Hemisphere?

A: The Battle of Gettysburg, fought July 1–3, 1863, involved more than 163,000 troops and resulted in approximately 51,000 casualties, making it the largest battle fought in the Western Hemisphere.

Q: What was the last battle in which Grant and Sherman fought together?

A: The two fought together last at the Battle of Missionary Ridge on November 25, 1863. Soon afterward, Grant dispatched Sherman on the Atlanta Campaign and assumed command as general-in-chief in Virginia.

Q: How many troops did Confederate cavalry commander J. E. B. Stuart lose in his famous ride around McClellan's army on the eve of the Seven Days' Battles?

A: On June 12–15, 1862, Stuart and 1,200 horsemen circled the 100,000-man Union army on the Peninsula near Richmond, destroyed numerous Federal supply wagons, captured 170 prisoners, covered approximately 150 miles—and lost one trooper.

Q: What 1862 battle had these landmarks: Little Sugar Creek, Keetsville Road, Leetown, Wire Road, and Elkhorn Tavern?

A: All were landmarks at the Battle of Pea Ridge, fought on March 7–8, 1862.

Q: How were Federal army surgeons handicapped at the Battle of Perryville?

A: Water was so scarce on the Union side following the battle that the surgeons treating the Federal wounded were unable to wash their hands for two days.

Q: Did Grant accept Lee's sword at Appomattox?

A: Lee did not offer his sword and Grant did not request it.

Q: What engagement was preceded by a battle of the bands?

A: On December 30, 1862, the night before the Battle of Stone's River, Union and Confederate musicians positioned within easy hearing distance competed with each other with performances of "Yankee Doodle" and "Hail Columbia" versus "Dixie" and "The Bonnie Blue Flag."

Q: What 1865 battle broke Robert E. Lee's defensive line at Petersburg, resulting in the fall of Richmond and Lee's withdrawal to Appomattox?

A: Five Forks.

Q: What state was the birthplace of General John C. Pemberton, the Confederate officer forced to surrender Vicksburg to Ulysses S. Grant?

A: Pennsylvania.

Q: Who amputated Stonewall Jackson's left arm after he was wounded at Chancellorsville?

A: Jackson's amputation was performed by four physicians—Dr. Harvey Black, Dr. R. T. Coleman, a doctor named Walls, and Dr. Hunter McGuire—with McGuire responsible for the actual amputation.

Q: What important event happened in the front room of the Liester house at Gettysburg at the end of the second day's fighting?

A: General George G. Meade held a council of war there, polled his corps commanders, and decided not to withdraw his army but to await a Confederate attack—which was launched and repulsed the next day.

FACT: The Battle of Yellow Tavern, Virginia, where Confederate cavalry commander J. E. B. Stuart was mortally wounded in 1864, derived its name from an old abandoned stagecoach inn—the Yellow Tavern.

Q: What Confederate fort near Savannah, Georgia, fell to Federal forces on April 11, 1862, following a two-day bombardment?

A: During a 30-hour period, more than 5,000 artillery rounds battered Fort Pulaski, above, the large masonry fort which guarded the entrance to the port of Savannah. After much destruction to the fort, its commander, Colonel Charles H. Olmstead, surrendered to Union General Quincy A. Gillmore.

Q: Who commanded the Union and Confederate forces whose clash opened the Battle of Shiloh at dawn on April 6, 1862?

A: The battle began when a Union reconnaissance patrol from General Benjamin M. Prentiss' division, which was led by Major James E. Powell, traded fire with Confederates from General William J. Hardee's corps, under the command of Major Aaron B. Hardcastle.

Q: Approximately 5,300 Confederates were killed or wounded in the frontal attacks made by Union forces at Fredricksburg on December 13, 1862. How many casualties were recorded by the Federal troops in the attacks?

A: Approximately 12,700.

Q: What 1864 battle featured the following landmarks: Blockhouse Bridge, Alsop House, the Po River, Brock Road, and the "Mule Shoe"?

A: All were landmarks at the Battle of Spotsylvania, fought May 8–19, 1864.

Q: What American town was occupied by Union and Confederate armies more than any other locale during the war?

A: Winchester, Virginia, held this distinction by changing hands 52 times during the war.

Q: What battle was launched with these polite words: "Bring up your men, gentlemen"?

A: With this gentle command, Stonewall Jackson turned his troops loose against General John Gibbon's Union forces at the Battle of Groveton during the Second Manassas Campaign.

Q: Who was Union Colonel Robert G. Shaw and why was his death newsworthy?

A: Shaw was the 26-year-old white commander of the 54th Massachusetts Colored Infantry. He was killed leading the unsuccessful bloody Union assault on Battery Wagner near Charleston on July 18, 1863. When the Confederates buried him in the same mass grave with his dead black soldiers, he became a hero to abolitionists in the North.

Q: What were the Confederate casualties in the Battles of Peachtree Creek, Atlanta, and Ezra Church—General John Bell Hood's unsuccessful sorties against the Union forces threatening Atlanta in July 1864?

A: In nine days Hood lost more than 13,000 troops, compared to Federal losses of approximately 6,000.

Q: At Gettysburg, what Union regiment, led by Colonel Joshua Chamberlain, withstood a fierce Confederate assault on July 2 and held Little Round Top?

A: The 20th Maine.

Q: Who fired the first shot of the Civil War?

A: The first shot of the war came at 4:30 A.M., Friday, April 12, 1861, when Captain George S. James, commander of the Confederate artillery at Fort Johnson overlooking Charleston harbor, ordered Henry S. Farley to fire a 10-inch mortar, beginning the bombardment of Fort Sumter.

Q: What Confederate general, the descendant of a French countess, "disappeared" during Pickett's Charge at Gettysburg?

A: General Richard B. Garnett of Virginia, related to Countess Olympe de Gourges of France, was missing and presumed killed in Pickett's Charge, although his body was never identified.

Q: What battle took the life of Union General Philip Kearny?

A: Kearny was killed at the Battle of Chantilly, during the Second Manassas Campaign, when he accidently rode into enemy lines during the night of September 1, 1862.

FACT: On December 20, 1862, Confederate forces led by General Earl Van Dorn attacked a Union supply depot at Holly Springs, Mississippi, captured approximately 1,000 Union prisoners, destroyed more than $1 million in Federal supplies, and forced Ulysses S. Grant to postpone his advance against Vicksburg.

THE TEN COSTLIEST BATTLES OF
THE CIVIL WAR

Based on total casualties (killed, wounded, missing, and captured)

1

Battle: Gettysburg   *Date*: July 1-3, 1863
Location: Pennsylvania
Confederate commander: Robert E. Lee
Union commander: George G. Meade
Confederate forces engaged: 75,000
Union forces engaged: 82,289
Winner: Union
Casualties: 51,112 (23,049 Union and 28,063 Confederate)

2

Battle: Chickamauga   *Date*: September 19-20, 1863
Location: Georgia
Confederate commander: Braxton Bragg
Union commander: William S. Rosecrans
Confederate forces engaged: 66,326
Union forces engaged: 58,222
Winner: Confederacy
Casualties: 34,624 (16,170 Union and 18,454 Confederate)

3

Battle: Chancellorsville   *Date*: May 1-4, 1863
Location: Virginia
Confederate commander: Robert E. Lee
Union commander: Joseph Hooker
Confederate forces engaged: 60,892
Union forces engaged: 133,868
Winner: Confederacy
Casualties: 30,099 (17,278 Union and 12,821 Confederate)

4

Battle: Spotsylvania   *Date:* May 8–19, 1864
Location: Virginia
Confederate commander: Robert E. Lee
Union commander: Ulysses S. Grant
Confederate forces engaged: 50,000
Union forces engaged: 83,000
Winner: Confederacy
Casualties: 27,399 (18,399 Union and 9,000 Confederate)

5

Battle: Antietam   *Date:* September 17, 1862
Location: Maryland
Confederate commander: Robert E. Lee
Union commander: George B. McClellan
Confederate forces engaged: 51,844
Union forces engaged: 75,316
Winner: Union
Casualties: 26,134 (12,410 Union and 13,724 Confederate)

6

Battle: The Wilderness   *Date:* May 5–7, 1864
Location: Virginia
Confederate commander: Robert E. Lee
Union commander: Ulysses S. Grant
Confederate forces engaged: 61,025
Union forces engaged: 101,895
Winner: Inconclusive
Casualties: 25,416 (17,666 Union and 7,750 Confederate)

7

Battle: Second Manassas   *Date:* August 29–30, 1862
Location: Virginia
Confederate commander: Robert E. Lee
Union commander: John Pope

Confederate forces engaged: 48,527
Union forces engaged: 75,696
Winner: Confederacy
Casualties: 25,251 (16,054 Union and 9,197 Confederate)

8

Battle: Stone's River   *Date:* December 31, 1862–
                             January 3, 1863
Location: Tennessee
Confederate commander: Braxton Bragg
Union commander: William S. Rosecrans
Confederate forces engaged: 37,739
Union forces engaged: 41,400
Winner: Union
Casualties: 24,645 (12,906 Union and 11,739 Confederate)

9

Battle: Shiloh   *Date:* April 6–7, 1862
Location: Tennessee
Confederate commander: Albert Sidney Johnston/
   P. G. T. Beauregard
Union commander: Ulysses S. Grant
Confederate forces engaged: 40,335
Union forces engaged: 62,682
Winner: Union
Casualties: 23,741 (13,047 Union and 10,694 Confederate)

10

Battle: Fort Donelson   *Date:* February 13–16, 1862
Location: Tennessee
Confederate commander: John B. Floyd/Simon B. Buckner
Union commander: Ulysses S. Grant
Confederate forces engaged: 21,000
Union forces engaged: 27,000
Winner: Union
Casualties: 19,455 (2,832 Union and 16,623 Confederate)

Q: What Confederate general captured Plymouth, North Carolina, and its Federal garrison?

A: Supported by the Confederate ironclad *Albemarle*, General Robert F. Hoke and a force of Confederates captured Union General Henry Wessells and his garrison at the river town in eastern North Carolina on April 20, 1864.

Q: At what battle, fought in Virginia's Shenandoah Valley on September 22, 1864, did Union General George Crook decisively defeat Confederate forces under General Jubal A. Early?

A: Following his advance on Washington, D.C., Early and his Confederates suffered defeat at the Battle of Fisher's Hill.

Q: What was the name of the large canal dug by Union forces on the James River during action near Richmond in 1864–65?

A: To enable Union gunboats passage around Confederate batteries on the James River below Richmond, General Benjamin F. Butler directed the construction of Dutch Gap Canal, which was excavated primarily by black soldiers in Butler's command. More than 66,000 cubic yards of earth were removed, but the canal was finished too late to be of serious military value.

Q: List the four Union expeditions against Vicksburg which bogged down in the bayous of the Mississippi from February to April 1863.

A: Grant's advance against Vicksburg in the early months of 1863 failed with the Duckport Canal, Lake Providence, Yazoo Pass, and Steele's Bayou expeditions. Not until the summer of 1863 did Grant capture Vicksburg.

FACT: The Battle of Brandy Station in Virginia, fought on June 9, 1863, was the largest cavalry battle ever fought in the Western Hemisphere. A total of 20,000 Union and Confederate horsemen engaged each other in combat. At battle's end the Confederate cavalry under General J. E. B. Stuart was badly battered but held the field against General Alfred Pleasonton's hard-fighting Federal horsemen.

Q: What Union officer kept Confederate troops at Gettysburg from seizing both Culp's Hill and Little Round Top, denying Robert E. Lee's army key positions crucial to victory?

A: While temporarily commanding the Union forces on the first day at Gettysburg, General Winfield Scott Hancock reorganized the shaken Federal defenses and protected Culp's Hill. On the second day he commanded the wing of the Union army which repulsed the Confederate drive to capture Little Round Top.

Q: What bloody Virginia battle, fought on June 3, 1864, was named for a nearby tavern which did not serve hot meals?

A: Cold Harbor.

(Library of Congress)

Q: Who surrendered the city of Atlanta?

A: On the morning of September 2, 1864, advance troops of Sherman's army under Union General Henry W. Slocum penetrated the heavily fortified Atlanta defenses, above, which had been evacuated by the Confederate defenders, and accepted the surrender of the vital rail center from Atlanta Mayor James M. Calhoun.

Q: Hawkins Farm, Dowdall's Tavern, Orange Plank Road, Germanna Plank Road, Talley's Farm, and Wilderness Church were landmarks at what battle?

A: Chancellorsville.

Q: Who commanded the unsuccessful Confederate defense of Port Royal Sound in South Carolina, which fell to Federal forces on November 7, 1861, and provided the U.S. Navy with a refueling station on the southern coast of the Confederacy?

A: Confederate defenses at the Battle of Port Royal Sound were commanded by General Thomas F. Drayton.

Q: What Virginia community was destroyed on August 7, 1861, by *Confederate* forces?

A: Upon hearing that Union General Benjamin F. Butler was planning to use the coastal village of Hampton to house escaped slaves, Confederate General John B. Magruder evacuated the community's residents and ordered their homes burned.

Q: What battle, fought on February 20, 1864, ended the Federal campaign to reclaim Florida for the Union?

A: At the Battle of Olustee, fought some 20 miles from Jacksonville, a Confederate force under General Joseph Finegan decisively defeated Union troops under General Truman Seymour, ending a U.S. attempt to subdue lightly defended Florida.

Q: What battle, fought on June 27, 1864, near Marietta, Georgia, resulted in defeat for General William T. Sherman, whose Union forces suffered more than 2,000 casualties, while inflicting fewer than 500 casualties on the Confederates?

A: Kennesaw Mountain.

Q: At what Virginia battle were six Confederate generals captured and who were they?

A: At the Battle of Sayler's Creek, during the Appomattox Campaign, Robert E. Lee lost almost one-third of his depleted army, and among those captured were Generals Montgomery D. Corse, Richard S. Ewell, G. W. C. Lee, Eppa Hunton, Joseph B. Kershaw, and Dudley M. DuBose.

Q: During the Battle of First Manassas, what civilian occupant of the Henry House was killed?

A: The elderly, bedridden Mrs. Judith Henry was mortally wounded when an artillery shell passed into her house and exploded.

Q: At what battle was the Union commander named Opothleyahola?

A: In December 1861, a force of pro-Union Creek Indians under Chief Opothleyahola engaged a force of pro-Confederate Choctaw, Creek, Chickasaw, and Cherokee Indians at the inconclusive Battle of Chusto-Talasah in Indian Territory.

Q: Which side suffered worse casualties in the Confederate victory at Chancellorsville?

A: Although the irreplaceable Stonewall Jackson was lost during the Confederate victory at Chancellorsville, Confederate casualties totaled 12,821, compared with 17,278 Union casualties.

Q: Following the Confederate loss of Chattanooga, who succeeded Confederate General Braxton Bragg as commander of the Army of Tennessee when Bragg resigned his command?

A: On November 30, 1863, Bragg was succeeded by General William J. Hardee, who temporarily commanded the army until Bragg's replacement, General Joseph E. Johnston, took command on Wednesday, December 16, 1863.

FACT: Vicksburg, Mississippi, the most important Southern city captured during the war, was surrendered to Union forces on Independence Day in 1863. General John C. Pemberton, commander of the besieged Confederate forces there, discussed surrender terms with General Ulysses S. Grant on July 3 and could have postponed surrendering until after the holiday. However, he believed his troops would receive better terms if he allowed Grant to capture Vicksburg on the Fourth of July. The fall of Vicksburg effectively reopened the Mississippi to Northern trade and split the South—just cause for Northern celebration of Independence Day.

Q: How many Union troops were killed in the action which resulted in the capture of Confederate President Jefferson Davis?

A: Early on the morning of May 10, 1865, as two regiments of Federal cavalry converged on Davis' camp near Irwinville, Georgia, the Union horsemen accidently opened fire on each other, killing two soldiers and wounding others.

Q: In March 1863, Ulysses S. Grant's troops were forced to make a hazardous night march in the Steele's Bayou Expedition in Grant's campaign against Vicksburg. How did the Federal forces see to find their way through the bayous at night?

A: They mounted candles in the muzzles of their rifles, which lit the way and enabled them to see their route as they marched.

Q: In what Pennsylvania town was Confederate cavalry leader J. E. B. Stuart almost captured?

A: On June 30, 1863, during the Gettysburg Campaign, Stuart attacked a force of Union cavalry in Hanover, Pennsylvania, was surrounded by a Federal counterattack, and escaped only by jumping his horse over a wide ditch.

Q: The West Woods, the East Woods, Bloody Lane, the Cornfield, Roulette House, and Dunkard Church were landmarks of what major battle?

A: Antietam.

Q: What two rivers were protected by Forts Henry and Donelson?

A: Fort Henry, which fell to Union forces on February 6, 1862, commanded a portion of the Tennessee River, and Fort Donelson, which surrendered on February 16, 1862, overlooked the Cumberland River.

Q: Why was Confederate General Nathan Bedford Forrest's victory at Okolona, Mississippi, on February 22, 1864, a bitter win?

A: Forrest's brother Jeffrey was killed in the battle.

Q: What was another name for the Battle of Champion's Hill?

A: The Battle of Champion's Hill, fought May 16, 1863, during the Vicksburg Campaign, was also known as the Battle of Baker's Creek.

Q: What military action occurred on November 29, 1861, near Los Angeles, California?

A: On this date a band of pro-Confederate partisans led by Daniel C. Showalter was captured by Federal troops after a nine-day chase.

Q: In what battle did cadets from the Virginia Military Institute help inflict a humiliating defeat on Federal troops under General Franz Sigel?

A: The VMI cadets were part of the Confederate attack directed by General John C. Breckinridge against Union forces at the Battle of New Market on May 15, 1864. Four days after the Confederate victory General Sigel was relieved of command.

(Library of Congress)

Q: What Southern capital was burned on February 17, 1865?

A: On this date Columbia, the capital of South Carolina, was set afire during its occupation by General William T. Sherman's army and more than half of the city was destroyed.

Q: Who were the opposing commanders at the Battle of Perryville?
A: At the Battle of Perryville, which ended the 1862 Confederate invasion of Kentucky, Union forces were commanded by General Don Carlos Buell and Confederate forces were commanded by General Braxton Bragg.

Q: What natural phenomenon contributed to the capture of Fort Henry by Federal forces on February 6, 1862?
A: At the time of the Union attack on the fort, the nearby Tennessee River was at flood stage and the fort was so flooded that a boat had to be used to accept its surrender.

Q: Name the battle fought among these landmarks: Bethesda Church, Shady Grove Church Road, Haw's Shop, and the Chickahominy River.
A: All were landmarks at the Battle of Cold Harbor, fought June 1–3, 1864.

Q: What two generals—one Federal, one Confederate—were killed in action on July 22, 1864, during the fighting for Atlanta?
A: On this date both Confederate General William H. T. Walker and Union General James B. McPherson died in battle during the heavy fighting around Atlanta.

Q: What Civil War battlefield included these sites: Franklin Road, Wilkinson Pike, Overall Creek, Nashville Pike, and Hell's Half-Acre?
A: Stone's River.

Q: What two American presidents fought at the Battle of Antietam?
A: Lieutenant Colonel Rutherford B. Hayes of the 23d Ohio and Sergeant William McKinley, also of the 23d Ohio, both saw action at Antietam—and both later occupied the White House.

Q: What Confederate fort at Drewry's Bluff near Richmond kept the USS *Monitor* and other Federal warships from attacking the Confederate capital until war's end?
A: Erected south of Richmond on Drewry's Bluff of the James River, Fort Darling survived Union attempts to destroy it and kept Union warships away from Richmond until the city fell in 1865.

Q: Who were the opposing commanders at the Second Battle of Fort Fisher, fought on January 13–15, 1865?

A: Fort Fisher, which protected Wilmington, North Carolina, the South's last major port open to European supplies, survived an abortive assault under Union General Benjamin F. Butler in December 1864. It finally fell in January 1865 after a massive naval bombardment from a fleet commanded by Admiral David D. Porter and an assault by troops of the Army of the James under Union General Alfred H. Terry. The fort was commanded by General W. H. C. Whiting and Colonel William Lamb, under the departmental command of General Braxton Bragg.

Q: How many soldiers remained in Robert E. Lee's Army of Northern Virginia when Lee surrendered at Appomattox?

A: Although Lee's army had once numbered more than 80,000 troops, by the time of the surrender at Appomattox in 1865, it had shrunk to a force of approximately 26,000 men, which faced a Federal force of more than 100,000.

Q: Where did Confederate General P. G. T. Beauregard spend the night after the first day of battle at Shiloh?

A: Beauregard, who had assumed command of the Confederate army at Shiloh after the death of General Albert Sidney Johnston, slept in one of the captured Union camps—in General William T. Sherman's bed.

Q: How many Confederate generals were casualties at the Battle of Franklin?

A: On November 30, 1864, 12 Confederate generals were listed as casualties. Five were killed in action, one was mortally wounded, five suffered lesser wounds, and one was captured.

FACT: The last serious land action of the American Civil War was the Battle of Palmito Ranch, fought on May 12, 1865, near Brownsville, Texas. In the brief action Confederate troops under Colonel John S. Ford repulsed a Union force led by Colonel Theodore H. Barrett.

Q: What was Ulysses S. Grant's first battle against Robert E. Lee?

A: Lee and Grant opposed each other in combat for the first time at the Battle of the Wilderness in May 1864.

Q: What was the northernmost Confederate land attack of the Civil War?

A: On October 19, 1864, a force of 26 Confederate soldiers who had made their way to Canada crossed the border and struck nearby St. Albans, Vermont, taking $200,000 from the town's banks and causing several civilian casualties in what was the northernmost Confederate land attack of the war.

(Library of Congress)

Q: What was the real name of Burnside Bridge, the span made famous by the Battle of Antietam?

A: This stone bridge across Antietam Creek became known as Burnside Bridge because of the bloody struggle Union General Ambrose E. Burnside's troops waged to cross it during the battle. The span's correct name was Rohrbach Bridge. When the shooting ended, Burnside learned the creek was so shallow his men could have waded across.

Q: What Confederate general was mortally wounded at Falling Waters, Virginia, during the Confederate retreat from Gettysburg?

A: During a rearguard action on the night of July 13, 1863, General James J. Pettigrew of North Carolina, who had distinguished himself in Pickett's Charge at Gettysburg, was mortally wounded and died four days later.

3 | WARRIORS IN BLUE

Q: Who was the last surviving Union general, and when did he die?

A: The last surviving Federal general was General Adelbert Ames of Maine, who died in Ormand, Florida, on April 13, 1933, at age 98.

Q: Who raised the first U.S. flag over Richmond when the Confederate capital was captured by Federal forces on Monday, April 3, 1865?

A: On this morning, Federal cavalry units entered Richmond in advance of the Union infantry, and a Massachusetts officer, Major Atherton H. Stevens, Jr., raised the first flag, a U.S. guidon, over the Virginia statehouse, where the Confederate Congress had met.

Q: Who was the youngest general in the Union army?

A: General Galusha Pennypacker of Pennsylvania, who enlisted in the army at age 16, was promoted to brigadier general by the time he was 20, and became the youngest general in the Union army—when he was still too young to vote.

Q: What was the average height of a Union soldier in the Civil War?

A: 5'8½".

Q: What happened to John Huff, the Union private who mortally wounded Confederate cavalry leader J. E. B. Stuart at Yellow Tavern?

A: Private John Huff, a 45-year-old Federal sharpshooter, reenlisted in the 5th Michigan Cavalry, fired the shot which mortally wounded Stuart on May 11, 1864—approximately two weeks before Huff was killed in battle near Haw's Shop, Virginia.

(Library of Congress)

Q: When did the name "Billy Yank" appear?

A: Unlike the term "Johnny Reb," which was frequently applied to Southern soldiers during the war, the term "Billy Yank" appears to have gained usage only after the war. Most Federal soldiers, like these 1861 volunteers of the 8th New York, were content to be called "Yank"—a term applied to Union troops by Northerners and Southerners alike.

Q: In what Union infantry brigade did each regiment carry a green flag?

A: In the Army of the Potomac's Irish Brigade, which consisted of Irish-Americans, each regimental color guard displayed the green alongside the national colors.

Q: What was called "tangle foot" and "oil of gladness" by Union soldiers?

A: Both nicknames applied to alcoholic beverages.

Q: What Union army corps was designated by a badge shaped like an acorn?

A: The acorn badge belonged to the U.S. XIV Corps, which saw action at Stone's River, Chickamauga, Atlanta, on the March to the Sea, and in the Carolinas Campaign.

Q: What Union general was known as the "Bull of the Woods"?

A: General Edwin V. Sumner of Massachusetts received this nickname because of his bellowing voice.

Q: What Union general was executed by Confederate guerrillas in Tennessee?

A: General Robert L. McCook of Ohio, a veteran of campaigns in Virginia, Kentucky, and Tennessee, was recovering from a battle wound when he was captured and murdered by a band of Confederate guerrillas near Decherd, Tennessee, in August 1862.

Q: Who was the commander of Camp Douglas, the notorious Union prison for 10,000 captured Confederates near Chicago?

A: For most of the war, Camp Douglas was commanded by Colonel Benjamin J. Sweet, a commander of Wisconsin troops, who had been wounded at the Battle of Perryville.

FACT: The first Union regiment to cross the Potomac River and advance into Virginia was the 12th New York Militia, which left Washington, D.C., on May 2, 1861, crossed the Potomac, and occupied an advance position in northern Virginia.

Q: Who received this pre-battle pep talk: "You volunteered to be killed for love of Country, and now you can be"?

A: Reluctant Union volunteers received these words of encouragement from General C. F. Smith, a crusty veteran of the Mexican War, prior to engaging the enemy at the Battle of Fort Donelson.

Q: Where did Union General Joseph Hooker get the name "Fighting Joe Hooker"?

A: During the Peninsula Campaign, the Associated Press slugged a story "Fighting—Joe Hooker," and copy editors at subscribing papers throughout the North used the slug as a headline— "Fighting Joe Hooker."

Q: What was the popular name for the 39th New York Volunteers?
A: The Garibaldi Guard.

Q: What Northern cavalry commander was called "Kill Cavalry" by his troops?

A: Hard-riding General H. Judson Kilpatrick, leader of Federal horsemen in numerous bloody engagements, was given this nickname by his soldiers for his aggressiveness and perhaps for controversial orders which resulted in high casualties.

Q: Why did Union Private James Dunlavy of the 3d Iowa Cavalry receive the Medal of Honor for capturing *one* Confederate prisoner at the Battle of Mine Creek, Kansas?

A: The prisoner Dunlavy captured was Confederate General John S. Marmaduke, whose nearsightedness caused him to mistake Dunlavy for a Confederate soldier.

Q: What was "Virginia Quickstep"?
A: Union troops jokingly coined this name to refer to diarrhea— the most common ailment in the Civil War army.

FACT: Of the estimated 2 million Union soldiers who served in the Civil War, 267 were executed by U.S. authorities. The largest number of executions, 147, were ordered for desertion. The remaining 120 were executed for murder, rape, or mutiny.

Q: What Union officer, a graduate of West Point at age 18, was promoted to general but chose to serve in the army without rank or pay?

A: General Herman Haupt, above, assistant engineer of Pennsylvania's railroad system at age 19, was made head of construction for the U.S. Military Railroads in 1862 and was appointed brigadier general a few months later. Interested in continuing his work on a northeastern railroad system as a civilian, Haupt declined the general's commission but continued to direct the military's railroad expansion without any official rank or pay for more than a year.

Q: What was Terry's Provisional Corps?

A: In January 1865, troops from the U.S. Army's XXIV and XXV corps were organized for an assault on Fort Fisher, North Carolina, and were named Terry's Provisional Corps for their commander, General Alfred H. Terry.

Q: Why was Union General George H. Thomas called "Old Slow Trot" by his troops?

A: The commander of the Army of the Cumberland at Lookout Mountain, Missionary Ridge, and Atlanta, Thomas was injured in a train accident early in the war and for months was too sore to ride faster than a trot. This condition led his troops to popularize his nickname, which had arisen from his deliberate gait as a West Point instructor.

Q: Hoping to receive a wartime officer's commission, a retired army officer waited for two days in the Cincinnati office of George B. McClellan, but McClellan did not have time to see him. Who was the officer McClellan ignored?

A: Ulysses S. Grant.

Q: What Union officer transformed the U.S. Army's inadequate medical system into an effective medical corps?

A: In 1862, Jonathan Letterman was appointed medical director for the Army of the Potomac and so effectively reorganized the army's medical system that in 1864 medical reforms based on his system were established throughout the Union army.

Q: Who were the Loudoun Rangers and whom did they chase?

A: The Loudoun Rangers were a special unit of Union troops recruited to capture Mosby's Guerrillas—but they were unsuccessful.

Q: Who ordered Confederate President Jefferson Davis shackled in manacles when he was imprisoned at Fort Monroe, Virginia, at the end of the war?

A: The manacles were permitted by a U.S. War Department directive, and they were ordered placed on Davis by the commander of Fort Monroe, 25-year-old Brigadier General Nelson A. Miles, who became famous as a postwar Indian fighter.

Q: Who were "Sherman's Gorillas"?
A: Soldiers from the Midwest in William T. Sherman's command referred to themselves by this name.

Q: How long did it normally take for the U.S. government to forward the pay of slain soldiers to their next-of-kin?
A: Sixteen months.

Q: What famous device was invented by Colonel Paul Ambrose Oliver of the 5th New York Volunteers?
A: Following the war, Oliver became an industrialist and invented dynamite.

Q: What prominent U.S. senator was killed at the Battle of Ball's Bluff?
A: On October 21, 1861, Colonel Edward D. Baker, a U.S. senator from Oregon, was killed at the Battle of Ball's Bluff when he led his troops into a Confederate ambush.

Q: What Union general headed the honor guard at Lincoln's funeral and also presided over the commission which tried the assassination conspirators?
A: Both duties were headed by General David Hunter of Illinois, who also had accompanied Lincoln on his inaugural journey to Washington in 1861.

Q: Who was the only Civil War general from Russia?
A: The only Russian general of the war was the Union's John Basil Turchin, whose real name was Ivan Vasilovitch Turchinoff and who was a graduate of Russia's Imperial Military School.

Q: Who was the Union commander at the Battle of Second Manassas?
A: General John Pope.

FACT: During and following the Civil War approximately 1,700 Union officers were awarded the brevet rank of general, which was an honorary commission designed to note special distinction in service.

Q: Troops from which states had the highest desertion rate in the Union army?

A: Leading in desertions in the U.S. Army were troops from Kansas, Connecticut, and New Hampshire, followed by New Jersey, California, and New York.

Q: What Federal regiment was named the "Bucktails" and how did it get that name?

A: The 13th Pennsylvania Reserves, also known as the 1st Pennsylvania Rifles and Kane Rifles, were called the "Bucktails" because new recruits were required to display the tail of a buck deer as proof of marksmanship. The regiment saw action at the Seven Days', Antietam, Fredricksburg, Gettysburg, the Wilderness, Spotsylvania, and in other battles.

Q: When President Lincoln relieved General George B. McClellan as commander of the Army of the Potomac in 1862, what did McClellan's soldiers do to prevent his leaving on the day of his departure?

A: They uncoupled his railroad coach from its train, insisting that he could not leave, and recoupled it only upon his orders.

Q: What prominent Union general was nicknamed "Spoons" and why?

A: General Benjamin F. Butler acquired the sobriquet "Spoons Butler" for his alleged habit of appropriating Southern silverware while serving as military governor of New Orleans.

Q: What Union general left his name to posterity as the label for a certain style of whiskers?

A: General Ambrose E. Burnside was noted for his style of muttonchop whiskers, which became known as "sideburns" in his honor.

Q: What postwar achievement marked the career of Union General Henry L. Abbot?

A: Abbot, who commanded the siege artillery in Grant's 1864 Virginia campaign, was a principal engineer in the construction of the Panama Canal and was greatly responsible for the development of the canal's famous lock system.

Q: By what other name were the 1st U.S. Sharpshooters known?

A: Commanded by Colonel Hiram G. Berdan of New York, the 1st U.S. Sharpshooters were also known as Berdan's Sharpshooters.

Q: Why was Union General Nathaniel P. Banks called "Commissary Banks"?

A: Confederate troops under Stonewall Jackson gave Banks the nickname in reference to the huge store of supplies Jackson's army captured from him during the 1862 Valley Campaign.

(Library of Congress)

Q: How many black soldiers served in the Union army during the Civil War and how much were they paid?

A: During the Civil War 166 black regiments were organized in the U.S. Army and, according to official reports, enrolled 178,975 black troops. For soldiers like these men of the 107th U.S. Colored Troops, the pay for most of the war was $10 a month regardless of rank—significantly less than the pay of a white private.

Q: What Union army official was known as "Rip Van Winkle"?

A: U.S. Ordnance Bureau Chief James Ripley was given this nickname because of his opposition to breech-loading rifles.

Q: How much was the enlistment bounty offered to new Union recruits by the U.S. government in 1863?

A: In October 1863, the Federal government tried to stimulate recruitment of troops by offering a bounty of $300 to anyone who would volunteer for a three-year tour of duty.

Q: What fate befell newspaper reporter Edward Crapsey after he reported a story unfavorably depicting Union General George G. Meade?

A: A war correspondent for the *Philadelphia Inquirer*, Crapsey was accused of slander by Meade, who had the newsman ridden out of camp sitting backward on a mule while wearing a sign describing him as a "Libeler of the Press." The major Northern newspapers retaliated by omitting Meade's name from every war story but those reporting defeats.

Q: In June 1863, a Union transport left Nashville with passengers banished from that city, was turned away from Louisville, and was then forbidden to dock at Newport, Kentucky. Why were the boat's passengers unwelcome in any port?

A: The transport vessel, which eventually returned to Nashville with its passengers, carried prostitutes who had been rounded up and sent away from the army camps at Nashville by army officials.

Q: What Northern officer was both a general in the U.S. Army and an admiral in the U.S. Navy?

A: A lieutenant in the U.S. Navy at the beginning of the war, Samuel P. Carter of Tennessee was attached to the U.S. Army as a brigadier general in 1861, saw duty as a cavalry and infantry commander, and after the war returned to naval service— eventually gaining the rank of admiral.

Q: By what name was the 6th Pennsylvania Cavalry best known?

A: The horsemen of the 6th Pennsylvania, who carried lances early in the war, were best known as Rush's Lancers.

Q: Who developed the plan to take Forts Henry and Donelson—the 1862 Union victories which made Ulysses S. Grant famous?

A: Capture of the forts evolved as part of a strategy promoted by General Don Carlos Buell, who advocated a Union movement into East Tennessee along the Cumberland and Tennessee rivers through Nashville.

Q: Where did Union officer Robert Anderson see action after he surrendered Fort Sumter?

A: Anderson, who was promoted from major to general following the surrender of Fort Sumter, saw no significant action afterward and was relieved from duty in October 1861, his health seriously damaged by the ordeal of Fort Sumter.

Q: What Federal general was captured at Murfreesboro, Tennessee, by Confederate General Nathan Bedford Forrest?

A: On July 13, 1862, having assumed command of the Union post at Murfreesboro only a day before, Union General Thomas T. Crittenden and his command were surprised and captured during a raid by Forrest.

Q: At the time he left West Point for the war, what was the academic standing of George Armstrong Custer, the flamboyant Union cavalry officer who was to become a general at the age of 23?

A: Custer, who was on detention for excess demerits at the time of graduation, was ranked last in the class of 1861.

Q: Who were "Tennessee Tories"?

A: The name was used by Confederates from Tennessee to refer to Unionists from Tennessee who joined the Northern army.

FACT: The Union army's XI Corps, which saw action at Chancellorsville, Gettysburg, and Chattanooga, contained so many soldiers of German extraction that it was popularly known in the army as the "German Corps."

Q: What was the first regiment of black troops mustered in the Civil War?

A: Union General Benjamin F. Butler organized the 1st Louisiana National Guard, the Union's first black regiment, in New Orleans in September 1862. The 1st South Carolina, another black unit, had been authorized near Beaufort a few months earlier, but the 1st Louisiana was mustered first.

(*Library of Congress*)

Q: What were the "noxious effluvia" which every Union soldier encountered in camp—much to the concern of Union physicians?

A: Crowded into huge camps like this one in Virginia, Federal soldiers were constantly exposed to "noxious effluvia"—a Civil War medical term for unpleasant odors—which Union surgeons believed harmful to health.

FAMOUS FACES IN BLUE

Identify These Union Generals

1 (Library of Congress)

2 (Library of Congress)

3 (Library of Congress)

4 (Library of Congress)

5 (National Archives)

6 (Library of Congress)

7 (*Library of Congress*) **8** (*U.S. Military History Institute*) **9** (*Library of Congress*)

10 (*Library of Congress*) **11** (*Library of Congress*) **12** (*Library of Congress*)

ANSWERS

1. Irvin McDowell
2. George Stoneman
3. George Armstrong Custer
4. Winfield S. Hancock
5. George B. McClellan
6. Benjamin F. Butler

7. Henry W. Halleck
8. Nathaniel P. Banks
9. Ambrose E. Burnside
10. Oliver O. Howard
11. George Gordon Meade
12. Judson Kilpatrick

Q: At the end of the second day's fighting at Gettysburg, General George G. Meade and his commanders held a council of war at Meade's field headquarters and decided to stay and fight. What did General Gouverneur K. Warren, Meade's chief of engineers, do during the meeting?

A: Warren, who had distinguished himself in the day's fighting on Little Round Top and had suffered a neck wound, lay down in a corner of the room where the war council occurred and slept through the meeting.

Q: Who was the first officer to command the U.S. Army Signal Corps?

A: The U.S. Army Signal Corps was established on June 21, 1860, and was first commanded by Major Albert J. Myer, a co-developer of the "Wigwag" signal system used by the U.S. Army, until he was reassigned to the Western theater and was succeeded by Major William Nicodemus.

Q: What Union regiments captured Confederate President Jefferson Davis?

A: On May 10, 1865, Davis and his family were captured near Irwinville, Georgia, by the 4th Michigan Cavalry and the 1st Wisconsin Cavalry.

Q: What famous Union general barely escaped serious injury— perhaps even death—in Mathew Brady's photography studio?

A: In March 1864, General Ulysses S. Grant was sitting for a portrait in Mathew Brady's Washington studio when one of Brady's assistants accidentally shattered an overhead skylight. The studio was showered with sharp, heavy glass, which somehow fell all around Grant without hitting him.

Q: What Union officer responded to a demand for surrender by seeking advice from the opposing Confederate commander?

A: Surrounded by a superior Confederate army at Munfordville, Kentucky, in September 1862, Union Colonel John Thomas Wilder, under a flag of truce, sought advice from Confederate General Simon B. Buckner, viewed the opposing force, then surrendered his command.

Q: Why was Union General Philip H. Sheridan known as "Little Phil"?

A: A veteran commander at Perryville, Stone's River, Chickamauga, and Missionary Ridge, and named commander of Grant's cavalry corps in 1864, Sheridan was 5'5" tall and weighed 115 pounds.

Q: What prominent Union military figure had been the prewar employer of General Ambrose E. Burnside, who commanded the Army of the Potomac at the time of the 1862 Battle of Fredricksburg?

A: Before the war Burnside had served as treasurer of the Illinois Central Railroad under George B. McClellan—whom Burnside reluctantly replaced as commander of the Army of the Potomac following the Battle of Antietam.

Q: What high-ranking Northern government official toured the captured Confederate capital of Richmond on April 4, 1865, and sat in Jefferson Davis' chair in the vacated Confederate White House?

A: Abraham Lincoln.

Q: Which Civil War battle claimed the life of the grandson of Revolutionary War hero Paul Revere?

A: Colonel Paul Joseph Revere, an officer in the 20th Massachusetts and a grandson of Paul Revere, was mortally wounded at Gettysburg.

Q: What was "bully soup"?

A: "Bully soup," also called "panada," was a hot cereal served with great frequency to Federal troops. It consisted of cornmeal and crushed hardtack boiled in water, wine, and ginger.

Q: Name the female Union spy who was captured by General Braxton Bragg's Confederates in Kentucky and was sentenced to be hanged.

A: Pauline Cushman, a professional actress, supplied Major General William Rosecrans' Union army with information about Confederate forces in Kentucky, was caught and sentenced to death by the Confederates, but was saved by a Confederate retreat.

Q: What was Salisbury Prison before the war and how many Union troops died there?

A: Located in Salisbury, North Carolina, the prison was converted from an old cotton factory and became the last stop for more than 3,000 Federal prisoners who died there in 1864–65.

Q: What was the prewar occupation of General Benjamin H. Grierson, who was made famous by Grierson's Raid in 1863?

A: Before the war Grierson was a music teacher and a storekeeper in Illinois.

Q: At Gettysburg, during the Confederate assault on Little Round Top, what did the 20th Maine do when its soldiers ran out of ammunition?

A: Charged with holding the extreme Union flank, and out of ammunition, the soldiers of the 20th Maine fixed bayonets and attacked, turning the Confederate assault.

Q: Before the war Confederate General A. P. Hill proposed marriage to a young woman named Ellen Marcy, who declined the offer. Whom did she later marry?

A: Union General George B. McClellan.

Q: What prominent Union general was known as "Old Fuss and Feathers"?

A: General Winfield Scott, commander in chief of the U.S. Army in 1861, was so nicknamed by army officers for his affection for pomp and ceremony.

Q: What was "embalmed beef"?

A: During the Civil War, the U.S. Army contracted beef from Chicago meat packers, who produced meat in tin cans for issue to Federal troops. The soldiers dubbed the stuff "embalmed beef."

FACT: The official pay for a Union private in the Civil War was $13 a month until May 1864, when the government raised privates' pay to $16 a month.

Q: Who was "Johnny Shiloh," also known as the "Drummer Boy of Chickamauga"?

A: He was John L. Clem, above, who left home at age 9 and became a drummer in the Union Army. His drum was destroyed by an artillery round at Shiloh. At age 12 he shot a Confederate officer at Chickamauga, later suffered two battle wounds, remained in the army after the war, and retired from the service on the eve of World War I as a major general.

Q: Of all the wartime commanders of the Union Army of the Potomac, whose command was the briefest?

A: The shortest command was held by General John Grubb Parke, who commanded the Army of the Potomac from December 30, 1864, to January 11, 1865, while General George G. Meade was absent.

Q: Who was the only general in American history to capture three separate armies?

A: General Ulysses S. Grant earned this distinction by capturing separate Confederate armies at Fort Donelson, Vicksburg, and Appomattox.

Q: Why was Union spy Elizabeth Van Lew called "Crazy Bet"?

A: Raised in a Southern family, Van Lew performed valuable intelligence work for the Union army in Virginia by pretending to be mentally ill, a subterfuge which earned her the nickname "Crazy Bet."

Q: What Northern political general, a former Speaker of the U.S. House of Representatives, was defeated by Stonewall Jackson during the 1862 Valley Campaign, was defeated again at Cedar Mountain, and commanded the unsuccessful Red River Campaign in 1864?

A: General Nathaniel P. Banks.

FACT: At the Battle of the Crater near Petersburg on July 30, 1864, a 500-foot-long mineshaft filled with 8,000 pounds of black powder was exploded under a portion of the Confederate lines. Plans for the mine were officially proposed by Lieutenant Colonel Henry Pleasants, a former mine engineer, and the shaft was dug by troops of the 48th Pennsylvania, who had been coal miners in civilian life. When the secret weapon was detonated, the explosion created a crater 30 feet deep, 80 feet wide and 200 feet long. It also caused 300 Confederate casualties, but the Union assault which followed was repulsed.

Q: What Federal general was nicknamed "Curly," "Fanny," and "Autie"?

A: The nicknames belonged to General George Armstrong Custer.

Q: How many votes did General George B. McClellan receive in the 1864 presidential election, in which he ran as the Democratic candidate against Republican Lincoln?

A: McClellan received 1.8 million popular votes and 21 electoral votes, while Lincoln received 2.3 million popular votes and 212 electoral votes.

Q: What was the official name of a common camp disease defined by Union army surgeons as a "temporary feeling of depression . . . on account of discomfort, hardships, and exposures"?

A: The "disease" was officially termed "nostalgia"—commonly known as homesickness.

Q: What Union officer commanded the victorious Federal expedition against Roanoke Island, North Carolina?

A: On February 8, 1862, Union General Ambrose E. Burnside and approximately 7,500 Federal troops captured Roanoke Island in an amphibious operation which gave the U.S. Navy a vital refueling station on the North Carolina coast.

Q: Who commanded the Federal forces at the Union victory at Nashville on December 15–16, 1864?

A: General George H. Thomas.

Q: Who was the first black officer to hold a field command in the Union army?

A: Major Martin R. Delany, a graduate of Harvard Medical School, was the union's first black field officer.

Q: What eventually happened to General John Buford, whose Federal cavalry stalled the Confederate advance on the first day at Gettysburg long enough for Union reinforcements to assume key defensive positions?

A: Buford survived Gettysburg but lived less than six months, dying on December 16, 1863, at age 37 from illness contracted in the field.

Q: What three Union officers were officially honored by the U.S. Congress for their actions at Gettysburg?

A: General George G. Meade, General Winfield S. Hancock, and General Oliver O. Howard all received the official Thanks of Congress for service at Gettysburg.

Q: What famous Union general was killed by Indians in 1873?

A: After accepting the surrender of the two remaining major Confederate forces in the Western theater in 1865, Union General Edward R. S. Canby became a departmental commander in the postwar army. In 1873 he was murdered by Modoc Indians while negotiating a treaty in California, becoming the only U.S. general in the regular army to be killed by Indians.

Q: What Union general accepted the surrender of Charleston, South Carolina, on Saturday, February 18, 1865?

A: A day after Confederates under General William J. Hardee evacuated the birthplace of secession, which had successfully resisted all Union attacks, Charleston city officials surrendered the port city to the troops of General Alexander Schimmelfennig.

Q: What Union officer was nicknamed "Old Probabilities"?

A: Major Albert J. Myer, the chief signal officer of the U.S. Signal Corps, earned the nickname for his accomplishments in the early science of meteorology.

Q: What Union general was known for always wearing clean shirts, despite the grime of battle?

A: The predictably neat attire was a trademark of General Winfield Scott Hancock, who distinguished himself in battle from the Peninsula Campaign to Petersburg.

FACT: The last Union officer killed in action in the Civil War was Lieutenant Edward L. Stevens of the 54th Massachusetts Volunteers, who was killed in a skirmish at Boykin's Mills, near Sumter, South Carolina, on April 17, 1865.

WARRIORS IN GRAY

Q: Who was the last Confederate general to die?

A: General Felix H. Robertson, the only Confederate general born in Texas, saw action at Shiloh, Murfreesboro, Chickamauga, and Atlanta; survived the war; and lived in Texas until he died in Waco on April 20, 1928—the last Confederate general to die.

Q: How fast could Stonewall Jackson's famous "Foot Cavalry" march?

A: Known for its ability to endure forced marches at a rapid pace, Jackson's "Foot Cavalry" once achieved a marching speed of almost six miles an hour—a remarkable speed for infantry.

Q: What Confederate regiment was known as the "Pelican Rifles"?

A: The 3d Louisiana Infantry.

Q: What was Confederate "cush"?

A: It was a stew dish composed of bacon, cornbread, and water, cooked together until the water was boiled out.

Q: How old was Confederate General John Bell Hood when appointed to the rank of full general?

A: Thirty-three.

Q: How old was Confederate General Joseph Wheeler when he assumed command of all cavalry in the Army of Tennessee?

A: Wheeler was 26 when he received the command. He was wounded three times during the war, commanded the cavalry forces of the Army of Mississippi, and eventually served as a major general in the U.S. Army during the Spanish-American War.

Q: What post was Jefferson Davis seeking at the time he was elected president by the Confederate Congress?

A: At the time of his election in 1861, Davis was commander of Mississippi's state forces and was hoping to receive a high military command in the Confederate army.

Q: What did Confederate General George E. Pickett—made famous by Pickett's Charge at Gettysburg—do after the war?

A: He was an insurance salesman in Norfolk, Virginia.

Q: Where did Confederate General Nathan Bedford Forrest receive his military education?

A: A naturally gifted cavalry commander, who became known as the "Wizard of the Saddle," Forrest began the war with no military training and less than a year of formal education.

Q: What was "Company Q" in the Confederate army?

A: The sick list.

Q: Who was the first commander of the Confederate Department of South Carolina, Georgia, and Florida?

A: This department was created on November 5, 1861, and was placed under the command of General Robert E. Lee, who was ordered to Virginia four months later and soon assumed command of the Army of Northern Virginia.

Q: What troops were characterized by this description: "They ain't worth a low country cow tick"?

A: A Confederate veteran of the Army of Tennessee so described the state-militia units brought into Confederate service.

Q: Who was the highest-ranking general in the Confederate army?

A: General Samuel Cooper, adjutant and inspector general of the Confederate army.

FACT: During the Civil War 425 officers held the rank of general in the Confederate army. Eight were full generals, 17 were lieutenant generals, 72 were major generals, and 328 were brigadiers.

Q: Who was Joseph Reid Anderson and why was he important to the Confederacy?

A: Although he served as a Confederate brigadier general until wounded in the Peninsula Campaign, Anderson was best known in the South as the president of Richmond's Tredegar Iron Works—the most important producer of cannon and machinery in the Confederacy.

Q: When Robert E. Lee prepared to invade Maryland with his army of 40,000 to 50,000 men, how many new pairs of shoes did his troops need?

A: According to the Charleston, South Carolina, *Daily Courier*, the Army of Northern Virginia was in need of 40,000 pairs of new shoes.

Q: What national political post was held by Confederate General Albert Sidney Johnston, who was killed at Shiloh?

A: From 1838 to 1840, Johnston was secretary of war for the Republic of Texas.

Q: By what name was the Confederate 8th Texas Cavalry commonly known?

A: Organized by Confederate officers B. F. Terry and Thomas Lubbock, the 8th Texas Cavalry was better known as Terry's Texas Rangers.

Q: What did Confederate General Jubal A. Early mean when he told his troops to "holler them across"?

A: Early referred to the famous "Rebel yell." When ordered to charge a Union force, Early's officers told the general the troops were out of ammunition, to which he replied, "Damn it, holler them across," believing the fierce "Rebel yell" alone could repulse the enemy.

Q: What Southern governor was mortally wounded in battle as a private?

A: George W. Johnson, provisional governor of Confederate Kentucky, went into the Shiloh campaign as a civilian military aide, joined the Confederate army as a private during the battle, and was later mortally wounded.

Q: What was the full name of Confederate General S. R. Gist, who was killed at the head of his troops at the Battle of Franklin?

A: A native of South Carolina and a graduate of Harvard Law School, Gist's initials stood for States Rights.

Q: What Confederate officer at one time challenged Stonewall Jackson to a duel?

A: While a student at VMI, General James A. Walker unsuccessfully tried to fight a duel with VMI instructor Jackson after discipline by Jackson resulted in Walker's expulsion. Years later, during the war, Walker and Jackson became good friends, and Jackson eventually promoted his former student to general and gave him command of the Stonewall Brigade.

Q: What Confederate unit adopted this motto: "Lincoln's Life or a Tiger's Death"?

A: Soldiers of the New Orleans Tiger Rifles went to war in 1861 with this motto printed on their hatbands.

Q: Who was the last Confederate general to die from combat?

A: General James Dearing of Virginia was wounded during the Appomattox Campaign and died on April 23, 1865.

Q: Where was Confederate cavalry leader John Hunt Morgan imprisoned during the war?

A: General Morgan, who led his troops on raids into Ohio, Kentucky, Indiana, and Tennessee, was captured on a raid in Ohio in 1863 and was placed in the Ohio State Penitentiary— until he escaped and resumed his command.

FACT: By the last year of the Civil War, marching along together in the Confederate army were gray-headed oldsters and boys who had never shaved. The Confederate military draft at first applied only to white males between 18 and 35, but by early 1864 the eligibility had been widened to include those from 17 through 50. Soldiers even younger and many who were much older also saw service in the Junior Reserves and Senior Reserves, which were organized by many Southern states.

Q: What two famous Confederate generals were accidentally shot by their own troops almost exactly a year apart, on almost the same battlefield?

A: General Stonewall Jackson was mortally wounded on May 2, 1863, at the Battle of Chancellorsville. General James Longstreet was seriously wounded on May 6, 1864, near the site of Jackson's wounding, during the Battle of the Wilderness.

Q: How many horses were shot from under General Nathan Bedford Forrest during the war?

A: Twenty-nine.

(U.S. Army Military History Institute)

Q: What was the Confederate army's 43d Battalion of Virginia Cavalry?

A: It was the official name of Mosby's Rangers—the quick-striking Confederate guerrilla force led by Colonel John Singleton Mosby, standing second from the left, who posed for this wartime photograph with his partisan rangers.

Q: What Confederate officer refused orders to burn Chambersburg, Pennsylvania?

A: On July 30, 1864, Confederate General Jubal A. Early ordered the residents of Chambersburg to pay a half-million dollars in ransom or have their town burned in retaliation for Federal destruction of civilian property in Virginia. When the demand was not met, Colonel William E. Peters of the 21st Virginia Cavalry was ordered to set fire to the town, but he refused. He was temporarily arrested and the town was set afire.

Q: How old was Confederate spy Belle Boyd when she first conducted espionage for Stonewall Jackson?

A: Boyd, who gathered information for Jackson during his 1862 Valley Campaign, began her espionage career at age 17. She fled to England in 1863, eventually became a professional actress, returned to the United States and died in 1900 at age 57.

Q: Who was the "Angel of Marye's Heights"?

A: Union *and* Confederate soldiers gave this name to Sergeant Richard R. Kirkland of the 2d South Carolina Volunteers, after he risked his life to carry water to wounded Union and Confederate soldiers at the Battle of Fredericksburg.

Q: What Mississippi general was killed leading Confederate troops in an assault at the Peach Orchard at Gettysburg?

A: A native of Tennessee who commanded Mississippi troops at First Manassas, Fredericksburg, and Antietam, General William Barksdale was mortally wounded at the head of his troops charging the Peach Orchard at Gettysburg on July 2, 1863.

Q: What Confederate general was known as "Old Jube"?

A: General Jubal A. Early of Virginia, a corps commander in Lee's Army of Northern Virginia, was known to his troops as "Old Jube" and "Jubilee."

Q: What property were the soldiers of Robert E. Lee's Army of Northern Virginia allowed to keep according to the terms of the surrender at Appomattox?

A: Troops who owned horses or mules could keep them, and officers were permitted to keep their side arms.

FAMOUS FACES IN GRAY

Identify These Confederate Generals

1 (Library of Congress)

2 (National Archives)

3 (Library of Congress)

4 (Library of Congress)

5 (Library of Congress)

6 (Library of Congress)

7 *(Library of Congress)* **8** *(Library of Congress)* **9** *(Library of Congress)*

10 *(National Archives)* **11** *(Library of Congress)* **12** *(Library of Congress)*

ANSWERS

1. Richard S. Ewell
2. P. G. T. Beauregard
3. Nathan Bedford Forrest
4. Thomas J. "Stonewall" Jackson
5. Jubal A. Early
6. D. H. Hill

7. William Mahone
8. A. P. Hill
9. John Bell Hood
10. J. E. B. Stuart
11. John B. Gordon
12. Braxton Bragg

Q: What prominent Confederate leader was blind in his left eye?

A: President Jefferson Davis.

Q: How many men did Lieutenant Dick Dowling of the Confederate Davis Guards command when he and his troops withstood the advance of 3,800 Union troops at Sabine Pass, Texas, on September 8, 1863?

A: Forty-seven.

Q: What Confederate general was assassinated in his headquarters?

A: On May 7, 1863, at his headquarters in Spring Hill, Tennessee, Confederate General Earl Van Dorn was assassinated by a gun-wielding civilian who claimed that his wife and Van Dorn were having an affair—a charge Van Dorn's associates denied.

Q: Who was chief of ordnance for the Confederates?

A: General Josiah Gorgas, noted for his ability to supply Confederate troops, was named chief of ordnance of the CSA in 1861.

Q: What Confederate general from Virginia was mortally wounded at the "High Water Mark of the Confederacy"?

A: The "High Water Mark of the Confederacy" was set at Gettysburg by the fall of General Lewis Armistead, who led his troops over the stone wall on Cemetery Ridge and pierced the Union line before he was shot to death.

Q: What Confederate general resigned as U.S. secretary of war to join Confederate service?

A: General John B. Floyd, secretary of war in the Buchanan administration, resigned his post on December 29, 1860, when President Buchanan refused to order the Federal troops to evacuate Fort Sumter.

FACT: At the Battle of Franklin on November 30, 1864, six Confederate generals lost their lives. Killed in action were Patrick R. Cleburne, John Adams, States Rights Gist, Otho F. Strahl, and Hiram B. Granbury. A sixth general, John C. Carter, was mortally wounded.

Q: What prominent Confederate general began the war as captain of the "Raccoon Roughs"?

A: General John B. Gordon of Georgia, a brigadier general by 1862 and a major general by 1864, entered Confederate service as captain of a company of volunteers from the Georgia mountains who were known by this name.

Q: About whom did Robert E. Lee say, "I can scarcely think of him without weeping"?

A: Lee so expressed his grief upon learning details of the death of Confederate cavalry commander J. E. B. Stuart.

(Library of Congress)

Q: What were the "Quaker guns" used at times by Confederate troops?

A: To deceive Federal forces into overestimating the size of the opposing forces, Confederate troops within sight of Union positions would sometimes trim logs into the shape of cannon, paint them black, and mount them in artillery positions. The Southerners jokingly called their creations "Quaker guns." Above, a Union soldier pretends to fire one of the fakes in an evacuated Confederate camp in northern Virginia.

Q: On what day of the week did Stonewall Jackson try to avoid battle?

A: Jackson, a devout Christian, would neither march nor fight on Sunday, if he could avoid it.

Q: Who said, "My poor boys! They were the noblest fellows that the sun ever shone upon"?

A: Robert E. Lee so described the soldiers of the Army of Northern Virginia in a conversation with a friend shortly after the war.

Q: What Confederate general did President Jefferson Davis consider as valuable as an army of 10,000 troops?

A: Davis placed such value on General Albert Sidney Johnston, who was killed at Shiloh.

Q: What was "pop-skull"?

A: "Pop-skull" was a Confederate term for contraband liquor, which was also called "bust-head," "rifle knock-knee," and "old red-eye."

Q: What made the 69th North Carolina distinctive among the Confederate troops from North Carolina?

A: It contained two companies of Cherokee Indians from the mountains of western North Carolina.

Q: What prominent Confederate general operated an Arkansas drugstore before the war?

A: General Patrick R. Cleburne, killed at the Battle of Franklin in 1864, was a professional pharmacist and half-owner of a drugstore in Helena, Arkansas, before the war.

Q: What nickname was given to Robert E. Lee following his first Civil War campaign?

A: After the unsuccessful West Virginia campaign in September 1861, critical Southern newspapers dubbed Lee "Granny Lee," which ceased to appear after the Seven Days' Battles.

Q: Who was described as a "seedy, sleepy-looking old fellow, whose uniform and cap were very dirty"?

A: Confederate General Stonewall Jackson was so described by a contemporary during the war.

Q: Who was governor of the Confederate Territory of Arizona?

A: In August 1861, Lieutenant Colonel John R. Baylor of Texas and 300 Confederates established the Confederate Territory of Arizona, and Baylor proclaimed himself governor—a post he held until President Davis removed him in 1862.

Q: What happened to Confederate General John C. Pemberton after he surrendered Vicksburg to Federal forces?

A: After a short period as a prisoner of war, Pemberton was exchanged; he resigned his commission as lieutenant general and served the remainder of the war as a colonel of artillery.

Q: What former U.S. senator from Alabama was imprisoned for alleged conspiracy in the Lincoln assassination?

A: Former U.S. Senator Clement C. Clay, a Confederate senator from Alabama during the war, was imprisoned without trial for a year on unproven charges that he had plotted Lincoln's murder while officially serving on a Confederate peace delegation.

Q: Where was Confederate guerrilla William C. Quantrill headed when he was mortally wounded by Federal forces?

A: The controversial Quantrill, who was mortally wounded in Kentucky on May 10, 1865, was reportedly en route to Washington, D.C., with plans to assassinate President Lincoln.

Q: What Confederate general from North Carolina commanded a brigade in Virginia and had a mountain named for him on the border of Tennessee and North Carolina?

A: General Thomas L. Clingman commanded a brigade at the Battle of the Wilderness and after the war spent much time exploring the Great Smoky Mountains, where Clingman's Dome is named for him.

FACT: The Confederate infantry regiment which suffered the highest number of casualties in a single battle was the 26th North Carolina. During fighting at Gettysburg, the regiment lost 708 of its 803 men, recording a casualty rate of almost 90 percent.

Q: Officers in what position were called "Yaller Dogs" by Confederate infantrymen?

A: Young staff officers who served as aides to senior officers were often recipients of this insult.

Q: What were "multiforms"?

A: This was the name Confederate soldiers sarcastically called their ragged uniforms while on the march in Lee's 1862 invasion of Maryland.

Q: What Confederate general was mortally wounded at the Battle of Bristoe Station?

A: On October 14, 1863, General Carnot Posey of Mississippi, a veteran of Antietam, Fredricksburg, Chancellorsville, and Gettysburg, was killed at Bristoe Station, Virginia, by Federal artillery fire.

Q: What name did Confederate soldiers give to the battle called Stone's River by Northern forces?

A: Murfreesboro.

Q: What Confederate general held the unlikely postwar posts of inspector general of the Egyptian army and doorkeeper of the U.S. House of Representatives?

A: General Charles W. Field of Kentucky, who saw action from the Seven Days' Battles to Appomattox, held a variety of jobs after the war, including the command in the Egyptian army and a brief stint as congressional doorkeeper.

Q: What was the real name of the violent Southern soldier who called himself "Charlie Hart"?

A: "Charlie Hart" was the alias used by the notorious Confederate bushwhacker William C. Quantrill.

Q: How many years of military service had been compiled by Confederate General John B. Gordon when the war began?

A: None. General Gordon, who commanded troops at Seven Pines, Antietam, Chancellorsville, Gettysburg, the Wilderness, Spotsylvania, Petersburg, and other battles, was in charge of a coal mine in Alabama before the war.

Q: What was "Kirby-Smithdom"?

A: The name was applied by Southern soldiers to the huge Trans-Mississippi theater of war, which was dominated by Confederate General E. Kirby Smith, above, for much of the war.

Q: After Confederate General J. E. B. Stuart's death in 1864, who commanded Stuart's Cavalry Corps?

A: Confederate General Wade Hampton.

Q: What was the Confederate Army of the Allegheny?

A: Troops under General Edward "Allegheny" Johnson in the northern Shenandoah Valley in 1862 were known briefly by this name before they were merged into the Army of Northern Virginia.

Q: What colorful Confederate general was nicknamed "Prince John"?

A: The nickname belonged to General John Bankhead Magruder, who earned the name with a reputation for princely entertaining.

Q: What were Robert E. Lee's favorite terms to describe attacks on the enemy?

A: In his wartime dispatches, Lee seldom used words like "crush" or "destroy," choosing instead to describe an attack on the enemy as a "blow"—his favorite term—or by the words "drive," "disperse," "harass," or "annoy."

Q: Who commanded all Confederate military prisons east of the Mississippi?

A: Confederate General John H. Winder, a former professor of tactics at West Point, held this post for most of the war, until he died while on an inspection trip to Florence Prison Camp in Florence, South Carolina, in February 1865.

Q: What postwar diplomatic post was awarded John Singleton Mosby, the famous Confederate partisan ranger?

A: After the war, Mosby supported Grant for president, joined the Republican party, and was appointed American consul to Hong Kong by President Rutherford B. Hayes.

Q: What was the Hampton Legion?

A: Shortly after South Carolina seceded from the Union, Columbia planter Wade Hampton raised six companies of infantry, four cavalry companies, and a battery of artillery—all at his own expense. He named them the Hampton Legion and led them to distinction at First Manassas.

Q: Who were "goober grabbers"?

A: Southern soldiers applied this name to troops from Georgia, whose zest for peanuts was famous within the Confederate army.

Q: What Confederate general, born in Kentucky and educated at Harvard, was the son of an American president?

A: General Richard Taylor, the commanding general of the Confederate Department of East Louisiana, Mississippi, and Alabama at the end of the war, was the son of President Zachary Taylor.

Q: What three high-ranking Confederate generals were baptized near the end of the war and what Confederate general baptized them?

A: In the spring of 1864, Generals John Bell Hood, William J. Hardee, and Joseph E. Johnston all prayed to receive Jesus Christ as Lord and Savior and were afterward baptized by Confederate General Leonidas Polk, who was also an Episcopal bishop.

Q: Who commanded the Confederate Army of New Mexico?

A: Active in operations in New Mexico and Arizona in 1861 and 1862, the Army of New Mexico consisted of approximately 3,700 troops and was commanded by General Henry Hopkins Sibley.

Q: What was unusual about Confederate Lieutenant Harry Buford, a company commander under General Barnard E. Bee at First Manassas?

A: Lieutenant Buford's real name was Loreta Velaques and she was a woman who had entered the Confederate army disguised as a man—a cover-up she claimed to have maintained for almost half of the war.

FACT: Hood's Texas Brigade, the famous Confederate unit which was engaged in major battles in both the Eastern and Western theaters of the war, was named for Confederate General John Bell Hood. Although the brigade carried Hood's name throughout the war, it was actually led by Hood for less than six months.

Q: What horse was General Albert Sidney Johnston riding when he was killed at Shiloh?

A: When mortally wounded at Shiloh, Johnston was atop a large bay horse named Fire-eater.

Q: What state post was held after the war by Confederate Chief of Ordnance Josiah Gorgas?

A: In 1878, Gorgas was named president of the University of Alabama.

Q: What Confederate colonel was dismissed from service by order of Jefferson Davis on charges of drunkenness, then was later promoted by Davis to general?

A: Colonel John Dunovant of South Carolina was dismissed by President Davis in 1862 for drunkenness on duty. He assumed a colonelcy in South Carolina state service and in 1864 was promoted to brigadier general by Davis for gallantry under fire— shortly before Dunovant was killed in action.

Q: What Confederate leader was described as looking "like a galvanized corpse which has been buried two months"?

A: A contemporary so described Confederate Secretary of War James A. Seddon, who was known for his unhealthy appearance.

Q: What Confederate general opened the fighting at Gettysburg and why?

A: Alabama troops of General James J. Archer's brigade, part of General A. P. Hill's corps and under senior command of General Henry Heth of Virginia, moved on Gettysburg at daybreak on July 1, 1863, and ignited the war's biggest battle. Unaware of a sizable body of Union cavalry in town, Heth had sent his troops to Gettysburg to capture a stock of shoes there.

Q: What were "gallinippers"?

A: Confederate soldiers called mosquitoes by this name.

Q: Who was the best-known cartographer in the Confederate army?

A: Jedediah Hotchkiss, a New Yorker who had come South before the war, became the Confederacy's most famous cartographer after he was commissioned by Stonewall Jackson as Jackson's principal mapmaker and was given the rank of major.

Q: How were these Confederate generals related to Robert E. Lee:
   Fitzhugh Lee, W. H. F. "Rooney" Lee, and George Washington
   Custis Lee?

A: Fitzhugh Lee was a nephew, and the other two Lees were sons.

Q: One of the five Confederate generals killed in action at the
   Battle of Franklin was General John Adams. How did he die?

A: Adams was shot to death at the head of his troops when he
   mounted the enemy breastwork on horseback during an assault.

Q: Who were "wagon dogs"?

A: Confederates who pretended to be ill and dropped back to the
   wagon trains to avoid battle were called "wagon dogs" by their
   fellow soldiers.

(Library of Congress)

Q: About whom was it said: "They were the dirtiest men I ever saw,
   a most ragged, lean, and hungry set of wolves. . . . Yet there was
   a dash about them that the Northern men lacked"?

A: An observer so described Confederate troops, like these men of
   the 9th Mississippi, during a hard march midway through the war.

Q: What Confederate artillery officer was the son of one famous American explorer and was named for another?

A: Colonel Meriwether Lewis Clark of Missouri, a West Point graduate who commanded artillery for Sterling Price and Braxton Bragg, was the son of William Clark and was named for Meriwether Lewis—the leaders of the famous 1804–1806 Lewis and Clark Expedition.

Q: What was a "galvanized Yankee"?

A: Union prisoners of war who enlisted in the Confederate army to escape the deprivations of prison life became known as "galvanized Yankees."

Q: Who was the youngest officer to be appointed general in the Confederate army?

A: The Confederacy's youngest general was William Paul Roberts of North Carolina, who enlisted in the Confederate army at age 19 and was promoted to brigadier general at age 23.

Q: For whom was Fort Donelson named?

A: The famous Fort Donelson, whose surrender launched Ulysses S. Grant's Civil War rise to fame, was named for Confederate General Daniel S. Donelson, who was a Tennessee planter and politician. He selected the site for the fort on the Cumberland River.

Q: What group of Southerners did Robert E. Lee lead after the war?

A: The Rockbridge County Bible Society.

FACT: A department of the Confederate army was equipped with more than 25 ships. Created in 1861 and charged with protecting the coastal waters of Texas, the Confederate army's Texas Marine Department used approximately 25 gunboats, transports, maintenance vessels, and barges in performing its duties.

5 | MEMORABLE DATES

Q: When did the Civil War officially end?

A: On May 10, 1865, President Andrew Johnson issued a proclamation declaring that "armed resistance to the authority of this Government in the said insurrectionary states may be regarded as virtually at an end."

Q: What important event occurred at Williamsport, Maryland, on Tuesday, June 16, 1863?

A: On this date Robert E. Lee's Army of Northern Virginia crossed the Potomac River near Williamsport, leading the Confederacy in the invasion that would end at Gettysburg.

Q: What was memorable about the photograph made of Abraham Lincoln on Tuesday, February 9, 1864?

A: It was the image later used on the U.S. five-dollar bill.

Q: On what date and day of the week was the Battle of Antietam?

A: Wednesday, September 17, 1862.

Q: What important wartime event occurred at 3:15 P.M., Sunday, May 10, 1863?

A: Confederate General Stonewall Jackson died.

Q: Why was February 11, 1861, noteworthy for Abraham Lincoln and Jefferson Davis?

A: Both left home for their inaugurations as president: Lincoln left Springfield, Illinois, for Washington and Davis left his Mississippi plantation for Montgomery.

Q: What Confederate fort on the coast of North Carolina surrendered to Federal forces on April 26, 1862?

A: Located near Beaufort, North Carolina, Fort Macon was surrendered by its commander, Colonel Moses J. White, to Union troops under General John G. Parke after a month-long artillery bombardment.

(Library of Congress)

Q: On what day of the week was the Battle of First Bull Run and for what was the battle named?

A: First Bull Run, also called First Manassas, was fought on Sunday, July 21, 1861, and drew its name from Bull Run Creek, above, which wound through the hilly northern Virginia countryside near Manassas Junction.

Q: What special deal did the Lincoln administration offer Union deserters on March 11, 1865?

A: Lincoln issued a proclamation giving all Federal deserters a free pardon if they turned themselves in within 60 days—failure to do so resulted in loss of citizenship.

Q: What major reorganization of the U.S. Army occurred on March 9, 1864?

A: On this date General Ulysses S. Grant was commissioned lieutenant general in a reorganization which made Grant general-in-chief of the U.S. armies and his predecessor, General Henry W. Halleck, the new chief of staff.

Q: On June 30, 1864, President Lincoln accepted the resignation of what prominent cabinet member with these words: "You and I have reached a point of mutual embarrassment"?

A: With this comment, Lincoln accepted the resignation of U.S. Treasury Secretary Salmon P. Chase, who had threatened to quit repeatedly because of differences with Lincoln.

Q: What controversial military decision did Jefferson Davis make on July 17, 1864?

A: On this date, Davis officially removed General Joseph E. Johnston from command of the Confederate Army of Tennessee, then defending Atlanta, and replaced him with General John Bell Hood.

Q: What Union admiral captured New Orleans on April 25, 1862?

A: On this date, after his warships ran the forts near the mouth of the Mississippi, Admiral David G. Farragut took them to New Orleans and accepted the city's surrender—closing the largest port in the Confederacy.

FACT: On August 8, 1863, following his defeat at the Battle of Gettysburg, General Robert E. Lee offered his resignation as commander of the Army of Northern Virginia to Confederate President Jefferson Davis, who refused to accept it.

Q: When did the last Confederate army surrender?

A: On June 2, 1865, Confederate General Edmund Kirby Smith surrendered the 43,000 troops of the Trans-Mississippi Department to Union General Edward R. S. Canby at Galveston, Texas—disbanding the last Confederate army in the field.

Q: When and on what days of the week was the Battle of Gettysburg?

A: The Battle of Gettysburg occurred on Wednesday, Thursday, and Friday, July 1–3, 1863.

Q: In what locality was slavery abolished on April 16, 1862?

A: On this date President Lincoln signed into law a bill passed by the U.S. Congress which outlawed slavery in Washington, D.C.

Q: What two prominent Southern statesmen died on July 26, 1863?

A: On this date former Texas president and governor Sam Houston died in Huntsville, Texas, and death also claimed former Kentucky senator John Crittenden, whose Crittenden Compromise had failed to avert war in 1860. Both men had opposed secession.

Q: What major wartime economic event occurred on August 2, 1861?

A: The U.S. Congress enacted the first national income tax on annual incomes over $800.

Q: What well-fortified Southern city came under extended siege by Union forces on May 18, 1863?

A: Grant's Siege of Vicksburg began on this date and continued until the vital river bastion fell on July 4, 1863.

Q: What made Saturday, March 18, 1865, a memorable date in the political history of the Confederate States?

A: On this date the Confederate Congress adjourned for what turned out to be its last official session in Richmond.

Q: When did Fort Sumter surrender?

A: At 2:30 P.M., April 13, 1861, Major Robert Anderson of the U.S. Army surrendered the fort to Confederate authorities after a 34-hour bombardment.

Q: What notable Union general—an accomplished astronomer—died of yellow fever on October 30, 1862, while in command of the Federal Department of the South, headquartered in Hilton Head, South Carolina?

A: General Ormsby M. Mitchell.

Q: What famous Civil War campaign was launched on November 16, 1864?

A: Union General William T. Sherman and his victorious army left Atlanta, beginning Sherman's famous March to the Sea.

Q: On what date was Fort Donelson surrendered?

A: February 16, 1862.

Q: How did Confederate President Jefferson Davis end the "bread riot" which occurred in Richmond on April 2, 1863?

A: When an unruly mob demanding bread began looting Richmond stores, Davis dramatically mounted a wagon, delivered a patriotic speech, threw the mob all the money from his pockets, then gave them five minutes to disperse before Confederate troops opened fire. They dispersed.

Q: What promotion did Robert E. Lee receive on January 31, 1865?

A: At the recommendation of Jefferson Davis, the Confederate Senate approved Lee's appointment as general-in-chief of the Confederate armies—a promotion made too late to allow Lee opportunity to make a significant impact with his widened authority.

FACT: On December 20, 1861, as regimental bands played "Dixie," two troopships of British soldiers left Great Britain bound for Canada, to be used in war against the United States. The troops were dispatched by the British government following the seizure of the British ship *Trent* by the U.S. Navy and the capture of two Confederate diplomats aboard. Diplomacy ended the crisis, however, and the British soldiers did not see combat.

Q: When was Jefferson Davis elected president of the Confederate States and who elected him?

A: On February 9, 1861, Davis was elected the provisional president of the Confederacy by delegates to the Convention of Seceded States, which met in Montgomery, Alabama, and which became known as the First Provisional Congress of the Confederate States. Southern voters confirmed the congressional decision with a general election on November 6, 1861.

(National Archives)

Q: When did Abraham Lincoln deliver his Gettysburg Address and how many people were present?

A: Lincoln made his brief speech on November 19, 1863, as part of the ceremonies dedicating the new soldier's cemetery at Gettysburg—an event attended by an estimated 15,000 people. In the photograph above, made at the dedication ceremony, soldiers with bayonets and dark-clad civilians crowd around the speakers' platform.

Q: To whom was this statement addressed on July 3, 1863: "Ah, General, you're in very great danger of being President of the United States"?

A: A Northern newspaper correspondent at Gettysburg directed this observation to General George G. Meade moments after Meade's troops had repulsed Pickett's Charge.

Q: What two Confederate generals were killed at the Battle of Pea Ridge on March 7, 1862?

A: On this date General Ben McCulloch and General James M. McIntosh were killed in battle within moments of each other.

Q: What battle, fought on May 16, 1864, ended Union General Benjamin F. Butler's offensive against Petersburg, Virginia?

A: After a two-week campaign, Butler's army was hit by a major attack from General P. G. T. Beauregard's Confederates at Drewry's Bluff on this date, forcing Butler to withdraw.

Q: At what battle, fought in northern Mississippi on September 19, 1862, did Union General William S. Rosecrans defeat Confederate General Sterling Price?

A: Iuka.

Q: To whom was this order directed on April 1, 1865: "Hold Five Forks at all hazards"?

A: On this date, as Lee began the withdrawal from Petersburg that would end at Appomattox, he used this dispatch to order General George E. Pickett to protect the Confederate right flank—an order Pickett failed to fulfill, and the Confederate line was broken at the battle of Five Forks.

Q: What disaster befell the Confederate navy on May 11, 1862?

A: On this date the famous ironclad CSS *Virginia* was blown up by her crew near Norfolk to prevent the warship's capture by Federal forces.

Q: When did Confederate General Joseph E. Johnston surrender the Army of Tennessee?

A: Johnston surrendered his army to General William T. Sherman at Durham Station, North Carolina, on April 26, 1865.

Q: What landmark event occurred on June 1, 1862?

A: On this date General Robert E. Lee assumed command of the Confederate forces previously led by General Joseph E. Johnston, who was wounded the day before at the Battle of Seven Pines. Lee named these troops the Army of Northern Virginia and led them as the main Confederate force for the rest of the war.

Q: When was the Battle of Valverde fought in New Mexico Territory?

A: February 21, 1862.

Q: What famous Civil War naval engagement occurred on June 19, 1864, off the coast of France?

A: On this date the USS *Kearsarge* engaged and sank the Confederate commerce raider CSS *Alabama*, ending a 21-month global cruise which had claimed more than 60 ships valued at almost $6 million.

Q: Who commanded the joint army-navy amphibious operation which captured Roanoke Island, North Carolina, on February 8, 1862?

A: The joint expedition, which captured the Confederate fortifications on the island and opened Albemarle Sound to Union forces, was commanded by Flag Officer Louis M. Goldsborough and General Ambrose E. Burnside.

Q: What Southern state capital was occupied by Union forces on February 25, 1862?

A: Following the surrender of Fort Donelson by the Confederates, troops under Union General Don Carlos Buell occupied Nashville, Tennessee, which had been evacuated by Confederate forces.

FACT: On August 17, 1862, the Santee Sioux in Minnesota, angered by conditions on their reservation, launched a month-long uprising which claimed the lives of an estimated 700 settlers and more than 100 Federal troops before order was restored.

Q: Against whom did the *Charleston Mercury* deliver this editorial on September 5, 1863: "He has lost the confidence of both the army and the people"?

A: Confederate President Jefferson Davis.

Q: In what two-day battle, fought October 3–4, 1862, did Confederate forces under General Earl Van Dorn fail to recapture a major railroad center in Mississippi?

A: Van Dorn's Confederates failed to dislodge Union forces under General William S. Rosecrans from their occupation of the crucial railroad center of Corinth, Mississippi, on these dates.

(Library of Congress)

Q: **What historic anniversary celebration occurred in Charleston, South Carolina, on April 14, 1865?**

A: **On this date the U.S. flag was again raised over Fort Sumter, four years to the day after it was forced down, and the officer directing the 1865 flag-raising, above, was the same Robert Anderson who had surrendered the fort to Confederate forces in 1861.**

Q: What controversial action was taken by Union General William T. Sherman on September 7, 1864?

A: On this date Sherman ordered the evacuation of the civilian population of Atlanta and, beginning September 11, some 1,600 citizens evacuated their homes and possessions in a move Sherman felt necessary to protect his army.

Q: At what battle, fought in northern Mississippi on June 10, 1864, did Confederate General Nathan Bedford Forrest rout a Union force under General Samuel D. Sturgis, capturing more than 1,500 prisoners and almost 200 supply wagons?

A: Brice's Crossroads.

Q: When and where was the Battle of South Mountain?

A: The Battle of South Mountain, a prelude to the Battle of Antietam, was fought west of Frederick, Maryland, on September 14, 1862.

Q: What major national event happened on May 4, 1865?

A: President Abraham Lincoln was buried in Springfield, Illinois.

Q: What veteran Confederate commander was killed in action near Boydton Plank Road at Petersburg on April 2, 1865?

A: On this date Confederate General A. P. Hill was shot and killed by a band of Federal stragglers as he rode across the field to rally his troops.

Q: What important naval development occurred at Long Island, New York, on October 25, 1861?

A: The keel of the U.S. Navy's first ironclad warship, the USS *Monitor*, was laid without ceremony on this date.

Q: What guerrilla commander was responsible for the Centralia Massacre of September 27, 1864?

A: On this date William "Bloody Bill" Anderson, a former Confederate lieutenant in Quantrill's Raiders, led a band of guerrillas on a raid into Centralia, Missouri, where they robbed a train, killed two civilians, executed 24 unarmed soldiers, and in a fierce skirmish killed all but 23 Union cavalrymen from an attack force of 147.

Q: When was the Battle of the Wilderness?
A: May 5–7, 1864.

Q: What Union general was mortally wounded at Antietam on September 17, 1862, just two days after he had received his field command?
A: On this date 58-year-old General Joseph K. Mansfield, commander of the Union XII Corps at Antietam, was shot and mortally wounded at the head of his troops.

Q: What battle, fought on July 1, 1862, was the final battle of the Seven Days' Battles?
A: Malvern Hill.

Q: What Union fort on the Mississippi River was captured by Confederate forces in a controversial battle that took place on April 12, 1864?
A: On this date General Nathan Bedford Forrest's Confederates successfully assaulted strongly defended Fort Pillow, capturing most of the fort's Federal garrison and reportedly executing prisoners—a charge Forrest denied.

Q: What major surrender occurred on May 4, 1865?
A: On this date Confederate General Richard Taylor surrendered the 12,000 troops of the Confederate Department of Alabama, Mississippi, and East Louisiana—ending all organized Confederate resistance east of the Mississippi.

Q: What famous American died on June 3, 1861?
A: Illinois Senator Stephen A. Douglas, the famous debater and former presidential candidate, died on this date of illness in Chicago at age 48.

Q: When and where was the first emancipation proclamation issued and who authorized it?
A: At his St. Louis headquarters on August 30, 1861, General John Charles Fremont drafted an unauthorized emancipation proclamation declaring freedom for slaves of all secessionists in Missouri—an act revoked as dictatorial by President Abraham Lincoln.

Q: What battle occurred in Arkansas on December 7, 1862?
A: Prairie Grove.

Q: On what date did the Confederate torpedo boat *David* severely damage the USS *New Ironsides* at Charleston with a spar torpedo?
A: October 5, 1863.

Q: When was President Lincoln's funeral and where was it held?
A: Funeral services for the slain president were held on Wednesday, April 19, 1865, in the East Room of the White House.

Q: What battlefield—the scene of bloody combat on December 13, 1862—was described in these words: "A chicken could not live on that field when we open on it"?
A: In a conversation with Confederate General James Longstreet, Edward Porter Alexander, Longstreet's artillery commander, so described the firepower with which he would soon decimate the Union ranks assaulting Marye's Heights at Fredricksburg.

Q: When did the surrender of Richmond, Virginia, occur?
A: Richmond, the Confederate capital, was officially surrendered to Union forces in Richmond's city hall at 8:15 A.M., on Monday, April 3, 1865.

Q: When did the Emancipation Proclamation take effect?
A: The Emancipation Proclamation, which was issued on September 22, 1862, became effective on January 1, 1863, and ordered all slaves to be freed in areas "in rebellion against the United States."

FACT: The last shot of the American Civil War was fired on June 22, 1865. On that date the Confederate commerce raider CSS *Shenandoah*, commanded by Captain James I. Waddell, encountered the Northern whaling ship *Jerah Swift* in the Pacific's Bering Sea and, to obtain the ship's surrender, fired one round from the *Shenandoah*'s 32-pounder Whitworth cannon—the last shot of the American Civil War.

Q: What prominent Confederate general was killed when his nearsightedness caused him to ride into Union lines at the Battle of Mill Springs, Kentucky, on January 19, 1862?

A: Former Tennessee congressman Felix Zollicoffer, a Confederate brigadier general, was shot out of the saddle by a Union officer when he mistakenly rode into Federal lines at the Battle of Mill Springs.

Q: What major Southern city and railroad junction was evacuated by Confederate forces on September 1, 1864?

A: Atlanta, Georgia.

(Library of Congress)

Q: What was the population of Sharpsburg, Maryland, site of the Battle of Antietam on September 17, 1862, and for whom was the town named?

A: Sharpsburg's residents numbered approximately 1,300 at the time of the fierce battle. The town was named for Horatio Sharpe, a governor of Maryland during the colonial period. Above, in a photograph made shortly after the battle, Sharpsburg's dirt Main Street slopes downhill.

Q: On what date and day of the week did Robert E. Lee surrender the Army of Northern Virginia at Appomattox Court House?

A: Lee surrendered on Palm Sunday, April 9, 1865.

Q: The sinking of what Civil War vessel on June 19, 1864, prompted this expression: "It is true we have lost our ship . . . but we have lost no honor"?

A: The sinking of the CSS *Alabama* was so reported by one of her officers, Flag Officer Samuel Barron.

Q: When did New Orleans, the largest city in the Confederacy, fall to Federal forces?

A: New Orleans was taken by Union forces on April 25, 1862.

Q: When was the Battle of Chickamauga?

A: September 19–20, 1863.

Q: When was the Battle of Missionary Ridge?

A: November 25, 1863.

Q: Who delivered this last line at Wilson's Creek, Missouri, on August 10, 1861: "Lehmann, I am killed!"?

A: Union General Nathaniel Lyon spoke these last words to an orderly seconds after suffering a mortal wound at the Battle of Wilson's Creek.

Q: What was the bloodiest single day of the war?

A: September 17, 1862, the day of the Battle of Antietam, was the bloodiest day of the war. At Antietam alone 12,410 Union troops were killed or wounded, and 13,724 Confederate soldiers were killed or wounded, for a total of 26,134 in a single battle.

FACT: On September 20, 1861, Union Colonel James F. Mulligan surrendered Lexington, Missouri, to Confederate General Sterling Price after Mulligan's 3,600 Federal troops held off Price's 18,000-man army for nine days. The Confederates finally captured the Union position by advancing behind wet bales of hemp.

Q: When did the first Southern state secede from the Union?

A: On Thursday, December 20, 1860, South Carolina's secession convention, meeting in Charleston, adopted the Ordinance of Secession and declared South Carolina an independent republic pending adoption into the Confederacy—an act which made South Carolina the first state to secede.

Q: Where was Ulysses S. Grant when his army was struck by the surprise Confederate attack at Shiloh on April 6, 1862?

A: When the early morning Confederate surprise attack occurred, Grant was eating breakfast at a house in nearby Savannah, Tennessee.

Q: When was the last major offensive launched by the Army of Northern Virginia?

A: On March 25, 1865, Robert E. Lee made a futile attempt to repulse Grant's army at Petersburg with a massive assault on Fort Stedman. The Confederates carried the fort but could not withstand the Union forces' counterattack and withdrew with a loss of 5,000 men—casualties of the Army of Northern Virginia's last major assault.

Q: What key Mississippi River island fortification fell to Federal forces on April 7, 1862?

A: Island No. 10, the principal Confederate fortification on the upper Mississippi, surrendered on this date to a naval force commanded by Admiral Andrew H. Foote.

Q: When and where was the Confederate Constitution adopted?

A: On the night of Friday, February 8, 1861, the Convention of the Seceded States meeting in the Alabama capitol in Montgomery unanimously adopted the Provisional Constitution of the Confederate States.

Q: On March 7-8, 1862, at the Battle of Pea Ridge, where did the Confederate commander establish his field headquarters?

A: During the battle Confederate General Earl Van Dorn, who was ill at the time, directed the combat from an ambulance. The Confederates lost.

Q: On what date and day of the week was the Battle of Shiloh?

A: Sunday and Monday, April 6–7, 1862.

Q: What Confederate fort, the last major fortification defending the entrance to Mobile Bay, fell to Union forces on August 23, 1864?

A: Fort Morgan was captured on this date, ending the blockade-running traffic at Mobile and leaving the Confederacy one remaining major port still open—Wilmington, North Carolina.

Q: What Tennessee city, occupied by Union forces on September 2, 1863, was a longtime target of President Lincoln?

A: Because of eastern Tennessee's strong Unionist sentiment, President Lincoln had been eager since the beginning of the war to seize Knoxville, Tennessee, which was occupied on this date by troops under Union General Ambrose E. Burnside.

Q: What nationally known Union officer was killed on May 24, 1861, after pulling down a Confederate flag from atop a boardinghouse in Alexandria, Virginia?

A: On this date Colonel Elmer E. Ellsworth, commander of the First Fire Zouaves and the leader of a famous zouave drill team, was killed by Alexandria innkeeper James Jackson, who shot Ellsworth after the colonel removed the flag from Jackson's inn. Jackson was killed by one of Ellsworth's men.

Q: What was the first joint army-navy victory of the war for the Union and when did it occur?

A: On August 28, 1861, Federal forces under Flag Officer Silas H. Stringham and General Benjamin F. Butler captured Fort Hatteras and Fort Clark on the North Carolina Outer Banks—setting a precedent for future joint operations.

FACT: Although Confederate forces had fired on the Union garrison in Fort Sumter three weeks earlier, the Confederate States of America did not recognize a state of war with the United States until May 3, 1861, when the Confederate Congress passed an act declaring war between the two governments.

Q: What climactic event occurred in Washington, D.C., on May 23–24, 1865?

A: For two days more than 200,000 blue-clad Union soldiers marched through the streets of the capital in a final military parade: the Grand Review of the Grand Armies of the Republic. The Army of the Potomac paraded on May 23, followed the next day by the seasoned marchers of Sherman's army. For more than six hours each day, the long line of victorious Union soldiers passed through cheering crowds and paraded by President Andrew Johnson's reviewing stand in front of the White House.

Q: What event on October 30, 1863, prompted this cheer: "The cracker line is open! Full rations, boys!"?

A: Surrounded by Confederate forces and surviving on starvation rations, Union troops besieged at Chattanooga were relieved on this date by Federal reinforcements who brought fresh rations and prompted this cheer.

6 | COLORFUL QUOTES

Q: What famous Northern figure said, "I failed, I failed, and that is about all that can be said about it"?

A: Abraham Lincoln used these self-critical words to dismiss his Gettysburg Address moments after delivering it.

Q: To whom was this compliment directed: "You got on sich a nice new-niform, you got sich nice boots on, you ridin' sich a nice hoss, an' you look like yer bowels wuz so reglar"?

A: At war's end a well-equipped, well-fed Union soldier received this admiring observation from a poorly equipped, war-weary Confederate soldier.

Q: What Civil War officer spoke these last words: "They couldn't hit an elephant at this distance"?

A: Union General John Sedgwick, a veteran commander at Seven Days', Antietam, Chancellorsville, Gettysburg, and the Wilderness, made this ill-fated prediction moments before he was shot and killed by a sharpshooter at Spotsylvania.

Q: What Civil War commander was described in battle in this manner: "He looked as though he ought to have been, and was, the monarch of the world"?

A: Confederate General Robert E. Lee.

Q: Who said, "You can sell almost anything to the government at almost any price you've got the guts to ask"?

A: A civilian contractor so described wartime dealings with the U.S. government.

(Library of Congress)

Q: **To whom did President Abraham Lincoln direct this rebuke: "Will you pardon me for asking what the horses of your army have done since the battle of Antietam that fatigues anything"?**

A: **Lincoln, above left, directed the remark to General George B. McClellan, above right, who had excused his lack of action against the enemy in the fall of 1862 with the complaint that his horses were tired. Soon after his comment, Lincoln removed McClellan from command.**

Q: Where did this high-ranking exchange occur?
"I turn the command over, sir."
"I pass it."
"I assume it."

A: With this conversation, the chore of surrendering Fort Donelson was passed from the senior Confederate commander, General John B. Floyd, to the second-in-command, General Gideon J. Pillow, who then passed it to General Simon B. Buckner. While Floyd and Pillow escaped, Buckner surrendered the fort.

Q: What battle prompted this vow from a participant: "I know I'm going home. I've had enough of fighting to last my lifetime"?

A: A Union straggler delivered this speech as he joined the Federal retreat from First Manassas.

Q: Who said, "By some strange operation of magic I seem to have become the power of the land"?

A: General George B. McClellan delivered this self-appraisal shortly after assuming command of the Union forces around Washington in 1861.

Q: About whom was it said, "We all felt at last that the boss had arrived"?

A: A soldier in the Union Army of the Potomac so reported his feelings when he learned General Ulysses S. Grant had assumed command of the army in 1864.

Q: What Civil War leader earned this description: "He will take more chances, and take them quicker, than any other general in the country—North or South"?

A: A contemporary so described Robert E. Lee.

FACT: Confederate General J. E. B. Stuart's last words were spoken on May 12, 1864, shortly before he died from a mortal wound received at the Battle of Yellow Tavern the day before. After asking two attending ministers to sing his favorite hymn, "Rock of Ages," Stuart made this statement: "I am going fast now. I am resigned; God's will be done."

Q: Who delivered this battle cry at First Manassas: "Look at Jackson's brigade! It stands there like a stone wall!"?

A: General Barnard E. Bee of South Carolina issued this famous description of Thomas J. Jackson's brigade at First Manassas. Bee was killed soon afterward and Jackson became famous as "Stonewall."

Q: Who boasted, "I fights mit Sigel"?

A: Thousands of German-Americans in the North rallied to the Union and joined the Federal army with this boast in order to serve as volunteers under German-born Union General Franz Sigel.

Q: Who said, "War is cruelty. There is no use trying to reform it. The crueler it is, the sooner it will be over"?

A: Union General William T. Sherman expressed this view shortly before beginning his devastating March to the Sea.

Q: Who said, "Well, I am glad to be done with guns and war"?

A: Union Admiral Andrew H. Foote made the comment upon learning of his impending death from complications of a wound received at the Battle of Fort Donelson.

Q: To what famous Northern figure was this blunt warning addressed: "Get down, you fool, or you'll be killed!"?

A: President Abraham Lincoln received this frank advice while under fire during Jubal A. Early's advance on the Washington defenses in July 1864. It was delivered by Captain Oliver Wendell Holmes, who would eventually become a U.S. Supreme Court justice.

Q: About what Union general was it said that "his headquarters are where his hindquarters ought to be"?

A: General John Pope became the butt of this joke when he publicly announced that his headquarters would be "in the saddle."

Q: Under what circumstance was this observation offered: "It's just like shooting squirrels, only these squirrels have guns"?

A: A Federal veteran so instructed new recruits in musket drill.

(Library of Congress)

Q: What Civil War general was described with this observation: "Boys, he's not much for looks, but if we'd had him we wouldn't be caught in this trap"?

A: A captured Union soldier so described Confederate General Stonewall Jackson, above.

Q: What Civil War military leader stated his philosophy of war with these words: "Find out where your enemy is. Get at him as soon as you can, and strike him as hard as you can. And keep moving on!"?

A: Ulysses S. Grant.

Q: What Civil War military leader stated *his* philosophy of war with *these* words: "There is always a hazard in military movements, but we must decide between the positions of inaction and the risk of action"?

A: Robert E. Lee.

Q: What notable Confederate general was described by a subordinate as "a tyrannical, hotheaded vulgarian"?

A: General Nathan Bedford Forrest.

Q: What prominent White House figure was described as the "Hell-Cat" by John Hay, Lincoln's assistant private secretary?

A: First Lady Mary Lincoln.

Q: What famous Confederate officer criticized Robert E. Lee's judgment at Gettysburg with these words: "That old man . . . had my division massacred at Gettysburg!"?

A: General George E. Pickett, who lost a majority of his division in Pickett's Charge, made this comment to Colonel John S. Mosby following an 1870 visit with Lee in Richmond. "Well," Mosby reminded Pickett, "it made you famous."

Q: What was the "Cotton Stealing Association of the United States Navy"?

A: Federal soldiers jokingly applied this imaginary name to the seamen and officers of the U.S. Navy at New Orleans, who seized civilian cotton, stamped it "CSA," then stenciled "USN" over the letters so they could claim it for sale as a prize of war.

Q: Who made this public statement on February 16, 1861: "The time for compromise has now passed, and the South is determined to maintain her position, and make all who oppose her smell Southern powder and feel Southern steel"?

A: Confederate President Jefferson Davis used this line in his inaugural speech.

Q: Who said, "I can make men follow me to hell"?
A: The daring, profane Union General Philip Kearny thus evaluated his leadership ability.

Q: Who wondered, "Do the generals expect us to be killed and want us to wear our burial shrouds"?
A: Confederates of the 2d Texas posed this question when they were issued undyed white uniforms shortly before the Battle of Shiloh.

Q: Who made this public statement on February 15, 1861: "There is really no crisis except an artificial one. . . . If the great American people will only keep their temper, on both sides of the line, the troubles will come to an end"?
A: President-elect Abraham Lincoln expressed this wishful sentiment in a speech at Pittsburgh, while en route to Washington and his inauguration.

Q: What high-ranking Union general was privately known to some of his subordinate officers as "a damned old goggled-eyed snapping turtle"?
A: General George Gordon Meade.

Q: Who made this boast before the Battle of Shiloh: "Tonight we will water our horses in the Tennessee River"?
A: Confederate General Albert Sidney Johnston made this unfulfilled prophecy shortly before the Confederate defeat at Shiloh.

FACT: The "unconditional surrender" message which made Ulysses S. Grant famous was someone else's idea. Grant's message to the Confederate commander of Fort Donelson, promising to "move immediately upon your works," if an "unconditional and immediate surrender" was not forthcoming, was suggested to Grant by General C. F. Smith, an Old Army veteran in Grant's headquarters. Grant sent the message, the fort was surrendered, and Grant became a national hero. General Smith's proposed message was less polite: "No terms to the damned Rebels."

Q: About whom did Abraham Lincoln make the comment, "I know the hole he went in at, but I can't tell you what hole he will come out of"?

A: Lincoln made this remark when asked the destination of Sherman's March to the Sea.

Q: What Union officer issued this terse command at Gettysburg: "Do you see those colors? Take them!"?

A: General Winfield S. Hancock issued this order to the 1st Minnesota on the second day at Gettysburg, as the Union line was being driven back. The Minnesotans responded by driving back the assault and capturing the Confederate colors—at a loss of almost one-third of the regiment.

Q: To whom was it said: "With this high honor devolves upon you also a corresponding responsibility. As the country herein trusts you, so under God it will sustain you"?

A: In March 1864, President Lincoln used these words to confer upon Ulysses S. Grant the highest rank in the army—lieutenant general.

Q: What Confederate general was publicly derided with the chant, "He's hell on retreat!"?

A: General Braxton Bragg of North Carolina, who led the ill-fated 1862 invasion of Kentucky and made controversial command decisions at Stone's River, Chickamauga, Chattanooga, and Fort Fisher, was often greeted by his troops with the jeer: "Bully for Bragg! He's hell on retreat!"

Q: Who told his quartermaster, "If you don't have my army supplied, and keep it supplied, we'll eat your mules up, sir"?

A: This warning was issued to an army quartermaster by Union General William T. Sherman prior to the departure of his army from Chattanooga toward Atlanta.

Q: What group was described by a Southerner as "the ugliest, sallowfaced, shaggy-headed, bare-footed, dirty wretches you ever saw"?

A: A Southern soldier so described the female camp followers lurking near his post in Alabama.

Q: What famous Civil War military leader made this statement to
    the chaplains of his army: "I can only say that I am nothing but
    a poor sinner, trusting in Christ alone for salvation"?
A: Robert E. Lee.

Q: Who said, "Really, Mr. Lincoln, I have had enough of this show
    business"?
A: Ulysses S. Grant so declined to attend a White House party in
    his honor in order to return to the front.

Q: About what battle was it said, "The Rebels are out there thicker
    than fleas on a dog's back!"?
A: An excited Union officer used these words to report the advance
    of Confederate forces at the Battle of Shiloh.

(Library of Congress)

Q: Who said, "The Rebel army is now the legitimate property of the Army of
    the Potomac"?
A: Union General Joseph Hooker, above, delivered this pronouncement
    shortly before he and the Army of the Potomac were defeated by Lee's
    Confederates at the Battle of Chancellorsville.

Q: What prominent member of the Lincoln administration was nicknamed "Father Neptune"?

A: Secretary of the Navy Gideon Welles was given this name by President Lincoln.

Q: What Union officer issued this final request: "Send for a clergyman, I wish to be baptised. I have been basely murdered"?

A: The words were spoken by General William Nelson, commander of the Union Army of Kentucky, moments after he was shot and mortally wounded by another Union officer, General Jefferson C. Davis, during an argument in Louisville in 1862.

Q: What were the last words spoken by Jefferson Davis?

A: "Pray excuse me. I cannot take it" were Davis' final words, spoken in response to his wife's attempt to give him medicine shortly before his death on December 6, 1889, at age 81.

Q: Who said, "This is a rascally world, and it is most hard to say who can be trusted"?

A: John Slidell, the Confederate minister to France, so expressed his frustration after unsuccessfully seeking official recognition of the Confederate States by French Emperor Napoleon III.

Q: Who boasted, "I'm going to take the cavalry away from the bobtailed generals.... I intend to make the cavalry an arm of the service"?

A: U.S. General Philip H. Sheridan made this vow soon after Grant brought him to Virginia in 1864 to command the Army of the Potomac's three divisions of cavalry.

Q: Under what circumstances was it said, "Hello, Massa; bottom rail on top dis time"?

A: A black Union soldier offered this greeting when he recognized his former master among a group of prisoners.

Q: Who said, "I shall do my best to save the army. Send more gunboats"?

A: General George B. McClellan, commander of the Union Army of the Potomac, telegraphed this message to Washington while on retreat from Richmond during the Seven Days' Battles.

Q: Who was described as "a self-made man who worships his creator"?

A: Horace Greeley, publisher of the influential *New York Tribune*, was so depicted by a contemporary.

Q: What were Stonewall Jackson's last words?

A: Jackson, who died of pneumonia after being wounded at the Battle of Chancellorsville, uttered these final words: "No, no. Let us pass over the river and rest under the shade of the trees."

Q: Who said, "Our Southern brethren have done grievously, they have rebelled and have attacked their father's house and their loyal brothers. They must be punished and brought back, but this necessity breaks my heart"?

A: The opinion was expressed by Major Robert Anderson, the Union commander of Fort Sumter during its 1861 bombardment.

Q: Who said, "It will be all right if it turns out all right"?

A: Ulysses S. Grant made this observation as he watched soldiers of his army storm Missionary Ridge near Chattanooga without orders.

Q: Who said, "It is well that war is so terrible—we should grow too fond of it"?

A: Robert E. Lee made this observation while viewing the carnage of the Battle of Fredricksburg.

FACT: Two days before the Battle of Gettysburg, President Lincoln appointed General George G. Meade commander of the Union Army of the Potomac to replace General Joseph Hooker, whom Lincoln had removed from command. Although Meade was selected for the important command primarily because of military and political considerations, one reason Lincoln chose him was because Meade was from Pennsylvania and Lincoln thought Meade would be especially determined to defend his native state from the Confederate invasion. Said Lincoln: "Meade will fight well on his own dunghill."

Q: Who said, "You are green, it is true; but they are green also. You are all green alike"?

A: Abraham Lincoln so described the Union army to its commander, General Irvin McDowell, while urging McDowell to attack the Confederates shortly before First Manassas.

Q: Who took this oath: "I shall come out of this fight a live major general or a dead brigadier"?

A: Confederate Brigadier General Albert Perrin of South Carolina made this pledge on the eve of the Battle of Spotsylvania, where he was killed in action.

Q: To what Federal general was this order given: "General, get up—dress quick—you are a prisoner!"?

A: General Edwin H. Stoughton received this command from Confederate partisan leader John S. Mosby upon being roused from his bed and captured by Mosby at Union headquarters.

Q: Who issued this victorious statement: "The Father of Waters again goes unvexed to the sea"?

A: President Lincoln used these words to declare his pleasure over the news that Federal forces had gained control of the Mississippi River in 1863.

Q: Against what order did Confederate General John Bell Hood officially lodge this complaint: "In the name of God and humanity I protest!"?

A: Hood expressed in this manner his opposition to General William T. Sherman's order forcing the residents of Atlanta to evacuate their homes and leave the city following its capture by U.S. forces.

Q: Who gave this order: "Lee's army will be your objective point. Wherever Lee goes, there you will go also"?

A: Ulysses S. Grant, newly promoted to lieutenant general and general-in-chief of the Union armies, gave this order to General George G. Meade, commander of the Army of the Potomac, upon Grant's 1864 arrival at the Virginia front.

Q: Who delivered this pledge and at what battle: "General, if you put every [Union soldier] now on the other side of the Potomac on that field to approach me over the same line, I will kill them all before they reach my line"?

A: Confederate General James Longstreet made this vow to Robert E. Lee as Longstreet's well-placed troops shattered repeated Federal assaults on Marye's Heights at Fredricksburg on December 13, 1862.

(Library of Congress)

Q: What soldiers were described with these unflattering words: "Some were drunk; many were insubordinate; others when detected with provisions or stores would not surrender them"?

A: A Federal surgeon recorded this description of Northern ambulance drivers at the Battle of Second Manassas—before the army's ambulance corps was reorganized. Above, a Union ambulance detail practices in preparation for battle.

Q: Who said, "Shoot, if you must, this old gray head, but spare your country's flag"?

A: No one. American poet John Greenleaf Whittier attributed the defiant statement to 95-year-old Barbara Frietchie, a resident of Frederick, Maryland, who allegedly delivered this line while waving an American flag at gunpoint before Stonewall Jackson's passing Confederates. The incident Whittier romanticized did not occur. In reality, the elderly Mrs. Frietchie sat on her Frederick porch and watched *Union* soldiers march by, while she held a small U.S. flag given to her by a relative. (Days before, as Confederate troops moved through the town, another Frederick woman, Mary S. Quantrill, did display a U.S. flag in their presence, but no one threatened to shoot her, nor did a poet memorialize her in verse.)

Q: "He looked more like a third-rate wagon master than a great general" described what prominent Union officer?

A: General William S. Rosecrans, who commanded the Army of the Cumberland, was so described for his casual appearance.

Q: "He will do nothing but run. He never did anything else" was said of what Northern military leader?

A: Union General Franz Sigel was so characterized by U.S. Chief of Staff Henry W. Halleck following Sigel's defeat at New Market in 1864.

Q: What Civil War officer proposed these terms to his opponent: "If you surrender you shall be treated as prisoners of war, but if I have to storm your works you may expect no quarter"?

A: Confederate General Nathan Bedford Forrest routinely issued this warning to opposing forces and often received his desired result.

Q: What war-torn region of the South was described by these words: "A crow would have had to carry its rations if it had flown across the valley"?

A: Virginia's Shenandoah Valley was so described by Union General Philip H. Sheridan after his devastating campaign through the region.

Q: About whom was it said, "It is of no use to re-enforce him, he is not going to fight"?

A: Confederate Secretary of State Judah P. Benjamin characterized Confederate General Joseph E. Johnston in this way shortly before President Jefferson Davis and his cabinet made the decision to remove Johnston from command during the 1864 Atlanta Campaign.

Q: What Civil War battle left a cornfield in this condition: "Every stalk of corn in the northern and greater part of the field was cut as closely as could have been done with a knife, and the slain lay in rows precisely as they had stood in their ranks a few minutes before"?

A: A Union officer who survived the Battle of Antietam so described the destruction of a Confederate force posted in a cornfield there.

Q: Who said, "I do not want to make this charge. I do not see how it can succeed. I would not make it now but that General Lee has ordered it and expects it"?

A: Confederate General James Longstreet in this manner expressed his reservations about Pickett's Charge to a colleague as Longstreet's troops moved forward to begin the famous assault at Gettysburg.

Q: Who said, "All this has been my fault"?

A: Robert E. Lee repeatedly spoke this line to the battered survivors of Pickett's Charge as they stumbled back to their lines in retreat.

FACT: Confederate General Nathan Bedford Forrest did *not* say, "Git thar fustest with the mostest." The statement is a misquote, which has been repeated in publications ranging from histories to liquor advertisements. What Forrest really said was that his Civil War campaigns were successful because he "got there first with the most men."

Q: Who said, "Jackson is driving us mad. He don't say a word—no order, no hint of where we're going"?

A: The frustrated complaint was made by Confederate General Richard S. Ewell in response to Stonewall Jackson's habit of keeping his battle plans in strict secrecy.

Q: What was the point of this wartime question: "Whoever saw a dead cavalryman"?

A: Civil War infantry troops frequently uttered this sarcasm in criticism of the cavalry, who were accused of fighting so rarely that they seldom left casualties behind.

Q: What Federal official argued against putting captured Confederate officers on trial for treason with these words: "If you bring these leaders to trial it will condemn the North, for by the Constitution secession is not rebellion"?

A: The opinion was privately delivered in 1865 by Salmon P. Chase, chief justice of the U.S. Supreme Court.

Q: What Civil War battlefield was so described by a veteran: "The dead covered more than five acres of ground about as thickly as they could be laid"?

A: A Confederate survivor so described the Union dead at the Battle of Cold Harbor in June 1864.

Q: What Civil War figure offered this advice and to whom: "Hold on with a bull-dog grip and chew and choke as much as possible"?

A: Union General Ulysses S. Grant was given this message of encouragement by President Lincoln during Grant's grueling Siege of Petersburg in 1864-65.

Q: What Federal officer ordered the sacking of Athens, Alabama, with this promise: "I shut mine eyes for one hour"?

A: The temporary loss of sight was experienced by Colonel John Basil Turchin, a former Imperial Russian officer who commanded the 8th Brigade of the Army of the Ohio in 1862, and who ordered his troops to loot and burn Athens as punishment for resistance by local guerrillas. Although temporarily dismissed for the action, Turchin was later reinstated as a brigadier by President Lincoln.

Q: What were Robert E. Lee's last words?
A: Lee, above, died at his postwar home in Lexington, Virginia, on October 12, 1870. His final words were: "Strike the tent!"

Q: Who said, "Success and glory are in the advance, disaster and shame lurk in the rear"?

A: Union General John Pope made this observation to his troops in a controversial speech shortly before the Battle of Second Manassas, where he was decisively defeated.

Q: Who said, "I don't care for John Pope one pinch of owl dung"?

A: Union General Samuel D. Sturgis, a veteran troop commander, made this comment during the Second Manassas Campaign.

Q: Who received these orders: "In no instance and under no circumstances, must you be beaten. . . . You will have energetic and watchful men to compete with. Eternal industry is the price of success. You must be active—very active. To be beaten is to be open to great censure"?

A: War correspondents from the *New York Herald* received these instructions from their editor.

Q: "It's all a damned mess! And our two armies ain't nothing but howling mobs!" described what 1864 battle?

A: A captured Confederate private so described the Battle of the Wilderness.

Q: Who said, "My religious belief teaches me to feel as safe in battle as in bed. God has fixed the time for my death. I do not concern myself about that, but to always be ready, no matter when it may overtake me"?

A: Stonewall Jackson.

Q: Who said, "I am now considered such a monster, that I hesitate to darken with my shadow, the doors of those I love, lest I should bring upon them misfortune"?

A: Robert E. Lee expressed this appraisal of his image to a friend a few months after the surrender at Appomattox.

Q: Who said, "General, unless he offers us honorable terms, come back and let us fight it out!"?

A: General James Longstreet so petitioned Robert E. Lee as Lee rode off to discuss surrender with General Grant at Appomattox.

Q: Who said, "The whole army is burning with an insatiable desire to wreak violence upon South Carolina. I almost tremble for her fate"?

A: General William T. Sherman made this observation as he prepared to lead his victorious army into the Palmetto State following his famous March to the Sea.

Q: Who said, "Stand by General Burnside as you have stood by me and all will be well"?

A: After being relieved of command of the Army of the Potomac in November 1862, General George B. McClellan issued this farewell advice to his troops—one month before General Ambrose E. Burnside led them into the disastrous defeat at Fredricksburg.

Q: What Federal officer sent this official message: "I am short a cheek-bone and an ear, but am able to whip all hell yet"?

A: Union General John M. Corse of Iowa made this peculiar boast in a message to superiors after sustaining a head wound at the Battle of Allatoona, Georgia, in October 1864.

Q: Who said, "Put not your trust in princes and rest not your hopes on foreign nations. This war is ours; we must fight it out ourselves"?

A: Admitting the Confederacy's failure to secure diplomatic recognition from Europe, Jefferson Davis so tried to officially bolster Southern morale.

FACT: After being forced to withdraw in the 1862 Peninsula Campaign, General George B. McClellan sent President Lincoln such an inflammatory dispatch that the U.S. War Department censored the message before Lincoln saw it. The deleted lines: "If I save this army now, I tell you plainly, that I owe no thanks to you or any other persons in Washington. You have done your best to sacrifice this army."

Q: Whose photograph was Abraham Lincoln examining when he said, "It is a good face. I am glad the war is over at last"?

A: Lincoln made the observation on the day he was shot when a prankster presented him with a photograph of Robert E. Lee.

Q: Who said, "I believe it to be the duty of everyone to unite in the restoration of the country and the reestablishment of peace and harmony"?

A: General Robert E. Lee made this statement following the cessation of hostilities.

Q: Who said, "I feel much better with this command than I did before seeing it"?

A: General Ulysses S. Grant made this comment after assuming the leadership of the battle-sore Army of the Potomac in 1864.

Q: Who made this observation: "We talked the matter over and could have settled the war in thirty minutes had it been left to us"?

A: A common Confederate soldier made this assessment after fraternizing with a Union soldier between the lines.

7 | THE WAR ON WATER

Q: Where was the Confederate States Naval Academy?

A: Created in March 1863, the Confederate States Naval Academy was established aboard the CSS *Patrick Henry* in the James River at Richmond. Cadets were selected by congressional appointment and occasionally left their studies to join in the defense of Richmond.

Q: Who picked the name for the famous Union ironclad *Monitor*?

A: The inventor of the vessel, John Ericsson, suggested the name, stating that the revolutionary ironclad would serve as "a severe monitor" to pro-Confederate European leaders; his suggestion was approved by the U.S. Navy Department.

Q: What did these Confederate ironclads have in common: CSS *Charleston*, CSS *Virginia*, CSS *Palmetto State*, CSS *Louisiana*, CSS *Neuse*, CSS *Tennessee*, CSS *Savannah*, CSS *Richmond*, CSS *Virginia II*, CSS *Wilmington*, CSS *Mississippi*, CSS *Chicora*, and CSS *Milledgeville?*

A: All were destroyed by Confederate forces to prevent capture by the Federals.

Q: What ship, built in Philadelphia in 1859, was originally christened *Habana*?

A: In April 1861 the *Habana* was purchased by the Confederate navy and was converted to the commerce raider CSS *Sumter*.

Q: What Union naval officer commanded the mortar flotilla used in the campaign against New Orleans?

A: Admiral David D. Porter commanded the mortar boats used to bombard Confederate fortifications below New Orleans, while overall command of naval operations against New Orleans belonged to Admiral David G. Farragut.

(Library of Congress)

Q: What Civil War naval cannon was nicknamed the "Soda-Water Bottle," and by whom was it invented?

A: The Dahlgren gun, developed by Union Admiral John A. Dahlgren, commander of the South Atlantic Blockading Squadron for much of the war, was called the "Soda-Water Bottle" because of its peculiar bottle-like shape. Dahlgren, above, poses beside his invention.

Q: What famous Confederate ironclad ram was built on the Roanoke River at Edwards' Ferry, North Carolina, and was commissioned on April 17, 1864?

A: The CSS *Albemarle*.

Q: What Union ironclad was sunk when Admiral Samuel F. Du Pont's nine-ship ironclad squadron attacked Fort Sumter on April 7, 1863?

A: During the battle between the Federal ironclads and Fort Sumter, the USS *Keokuk* sustained 90 hits, including almost 20 below the waterline, and as a result of the damage sank off Charleston the next day.

Q: What happened to Lieutenant William B. Cushing, the daring young Union naval officer who sank the famous Confederate ironclad CSS *Albemarle* with a spar torpedo?

A: Cushing, who led the boat crew that sank the fearsome warship in North Carolina's Roanoke River, died of a neurological disease in Washington's Government Hospital for the Insane on December 17, 1874.

Q: What powerful Confederate ironclad ram was owned by six nations under at least four names?

A: The CSS *Stonewall* was built for the Confederacy by a French shipbuilder under the name *Sphinx*. Because of diplomatic pressure from the United States, the builder sold the ship to Denmark, but Danish officials changed their minds and refused acceptance. The *Stonewall* was then sold to the Confederacy disguised as the *Staer Kodder*, but en route to America to break the blockade at Wilmington, the ship's commander learned the war was over. He sold the ship to Cuba, which gave her to the United States, who sold her to the Japanese navy—where she became the Japanese warship *Azuma*.

FACT: In 1861, blockade runners using Southern ports had a one-in-ten chance of being captured by the Federal warships blockading the Confederate coast. By late 1864, however, the odds for blockade runners had dropped to one in three.

Q: Why were ashes routinely spread on the decks of Federal warships going into battle?

A: The ashes were designed to prevent seamen from slipping on blood during battle.

Q: Where was the autopsy performed on the body of assassin John Wilkes Booth?

A: After he was shot and killed in northern Virginia, Booth's body was brought back to Washington, where an official autopsy was performed aboard the Union monitor *Montauk*, anchored at Washington Navy Yard.

Q: What was important about the launching of the British-built ship *Enrica* at Liverpool, England, on July 29, 1862?

A: Built for the Confederacy at Laird's Dockyard in Liverpool, the *Enrica* was commissioned at sea a month later as the CSS *Alabama*—the most famous of the Confederate commerce raiders.

Q: What landlocked North Carolina town had a naval yard which produced gun carriages and artillery projectiles for Confederate ironclads?

A: The Confederate Navy Yard in Charlotte, North Carolina, established in 1864, manufactured equipment for arming ironclads until the end of the war.

Q: How many miles were navigated by the Confederate raider *Shenandoah* during the war?

A: In 13 months, the *Shenandoah* had cruised more than 58,000 miles and had entered every ocean except the Antarctic, before finally striking her flag at Liverpool, England, on November 6, 1865.

Q: Where was the Confederate submarine *H. L. Hunley* built?

A: The *Hunley*, destined to become the first submarine to sink a ship in combat, was built from a cylindrical steam boiler in the Park and Lyons Machine Shop in Mobile, Alabama, in 1861 and was later transferred to Charleston for use against the Federal fleet besieging that port.

Q: Who was secretary of the navy for the Confederacy?
A: Stephen R. Mallory, a former U.S. senator and U.S. secretary of the navy, was appointed secretary of the navy for the C.S.A. in February 1861 and held the post throughout the war.

Q: What prominent Union naval officer was the son of a U.S. commodore, the brother of a famous Union admiral, the foster brother of another acclaimed Union admiral, the cousin of a prominent Union general—yet had two sons fighting for the Confederacy?
A: Union Commodore William Porter was the son of prewar commodore David Porter, the brother of Admiral David Dixon Porter, the foster brother of Admiral David G. Farragut, the cousin of Union General Fitz-John Porter—and the father of two Confederates.

Q: How many black seamen served in the Union navy?
A: An estimated 20,000 black sailors saw duty in the U.S. Navy during the war.

Q: What politician persuaded Abraham Lincoln to give the cabinet post of secretary of the navy to Gideon Welles?
A: Welles, the primary naval strategist for the Union during the war, was promoted enthusiastically to President-elect Lincoln late in 1860 by Vice President-elect Hannibal Hamlin.

Q: What distinction does the Union ship *Fanny* hold in naval history?
A: On August 3, 1861, balloonist John La Mountain observed Confederate batteries on Sewell's Point, Virginia, from a hot-air balloon launched from the *Fanny*—the U.S. Navy's first aircraft carrier.

FACT: The engine room of a Union warship with steam up could reach a temperature of 150°—hot enough to crack lantern glass and make metal machinery too hot for unprotected hands to touch.

Q: Who was the highest-ranking officer in the Confederate navy?

A: Admiral Franklin Buchanan, the first superintendent of the U.S. Naval Academy, then commander of the ironclad CSS *Virginia*, was the highest-ranking officer in the C.S. Navy.

(Library of Congress)

Q: What naval operation required the largest fleet of the Civil War and produced the war's largest naval bombardment?

A: The joint army-navy expedition against Fort Fisher, the huge Confederate fort at the entrance of the Cape Fear River near Wilmington, North Carolina, mounted the largest fleet of the war—64 naval warships and numerous troop transports. Never before had the U.S. Navy assembled so many ships for a single engagement. The fleet fired 20,271 artillery rounds into the fort on December 24–25, 1864—the largest bombardment of the war—and returned on January 13–15, 1865, to fire 19,682 additional rounds into the fortification. Fort Fisher surrendered on January 15, 1865.

Q: What branch of the Confederate military service was established by the Confederate States Congress on March 16, 1861?

A: An act of Congress on this date and another legislative act on May 20 established and organized the Confederate States Marine Corps.

Q: What popular naval ration was outlawed by the U.S. Congress in July 1862?

A: To the distress of many Union seamen, Congress forbade the "spirit ration" of whiskey at this time.

Q: Who guarded President Lincoln when he toured the captured Confederate capital on April 4, 1865?

A: Lincoln reached fallen Richmond aboard a boat from the USS *Malvern*, Admiral David D. Porter's flagship, and he was escorted through the captured city by ten of Porter's sailors, who were armed with carbines.

Q: On July 16, 1863, a U.S. warship fought a naval battle with the armed forces of a foreign power. What was the ship and who was it fighting?

A: On this date, the USS *Wyoming* engaged in battle with Japanese land and sea forces in the Shimonoseki Strait near Yokohama, after the Japanese government had threatened resident foreigners. The action was the first combat between the United States and Japan and the *Wyoming* was victorious.

Q: What Union admiral commanded the naval force which captured Port Royal Sound in South Carolina?

A: On November 7, 1861, a Union fleet of 17 warships under Admiral Samuel F. Du Pont bombarded the Confederate forts defending Port Royal Sound, forcing their surrender and capturing the region as a Union refueling station.

Q: What European nation built a fleet of 12 ironclads based on plans of the Union *Monitor*?

A: After sending an official observer to watch the construction of *Monitor*-class warships, Czar Alexander II of Russia ordered the construction of a fleet of 12 *Monitor*-class Russian warships.

Q: What action ended Confederate naval operations east of the Mississippi?

A: On April 3, 1865, under orders from Confederate Navy Secretary Stephen R. Mallory, Admiral Raphael Semmes scuttled the Confederate ironclads *Virginia II, Fredricksburg,* and *Richmond,* and the other ships of the James River Squadron near Richmond—conducting the last act afloat of Confederate naval forces east of the Mississippi.

Q: How many casualties did it cost the U.S. Navy to capture the Confederacy's largest port, New Orleans, considered to be the gateway to the Mississippi?

A: The taking of New Orleans cost the navy 36 dead and 135 wounded.

Q: How many ships were captured or destroyed by the Confederate raider *Georgia?*

A: In a career that lasted barely a year, the CSS *Georgia* captured or destroyed nine Union vessels.

Q: What happened to the Union naval officer who captured Galveston?

A: In October 1862 a flotilla of Union warships under Commander W. B. Renshaw captured the port of Galveston, but the port was recaptured in January 1863 and Renshaw was accidentally killed in an explosion as he tried to destroy his ship.

Q: What vessel towed the Union ironclad *Monitor* to the famous duel of ironclads at Hampton Roads, Virginia?

A: The *Monitor* was towed from New York City to do battle at Hampton Roads by the tugboat *Seth Low.*

FACT: Raising the hull of the scuttled USS *Merrimack* and converting the former U.S. warship into the Confederate ironclad CSS *Virginia*—the warship which battled the famous USS *Monitor*—cost the Confederate government approximately $6,000.

Q: What historical "first" was achieved by escaped slave Robert Blake?

A: After escaping slavery, Blake became a crewman on the USS *Marblehead* and on Christmas Day 1863, in an engagement between the *Marblehead* and Confederate shore batteries near Charleston, Blake distinguished himself serving on one of the *Marblehead*'s gun crews—an act which made him the first black man to receive the U.S. Medal of Honor.

(National Archives)

Q: **What was the *David*-class torpedo boat and who invented her?**

A: In 1863 a Charleston, South Carolina, shipbuilder, Theodore Stoney, built a semisubmersible boat which was armed with a spar torpedo. The original *David* attacked the Union warships *New Ironsides*, *Memphis*, and *Wabash* off the South Carolina coast in 1863–64. An undetermined number of similar torpedo boats were built in the South and, like this one photographed in Charleston at war's end, they all became known by the class name *David*, named presumably for the giant-slayer of Biblical fame.

Q: What revolutionary event in naval warfare occurred on February 17, 1864?

A: On this date the Confederate submarine *H. L. Hunley* sank the Union warship USS *Housatonic* off Charleston, South Carolina— the first ship ever sunk in combat by a submarine.

Q: What were the flagships of the opposing Union and Confederate naval forces at the Battle of Mobile Bay on August 5, 1864?

A: Union Admiral David G. Farragut commanded the Federal naval forces from the flagship USS *Hartford*, while Confederate Admiral Franklin Buchanan, who was wounded and captured in the battle, commanded the Confederate naval defense from the CSS *Tennessee*, which was also captured.

Q: Who was "Trenholm" in Fraser, Trenholm & Co., the British shipping firm so active in wartime blockade running?

A: Headquartered in Liverpool with an office in Charleston, Fraser, Trenholm & Co. was half-owned by Confederate Treasury Secretary George Trenholm.

Q: What two Confederate warships forced the Union flotilla to withdraw from Galveston, Texas, allowing Confederate forces to reoccupy the port?

A: On January 1, 1863, the CSS *Bayou City* and CSS *Neptune* surprised the Federal warships at Galveston, destroying the USS *Westfield*, capturing the USS *Harriet Lane*, and forcing the Union troops out of Galveston.

Q: What joint army-navy operation was described as "a ridiculous fizzle" by the *New York Herald?*

A: The newspaper so labeled the unsuccessful expedition against Fort Fisher in December 1864, in which General Benjamin F. Butler attempted to overpower the huge Confederate fort by exploding an old warship filled with powder.

Q: Who was the first Union naval officer killed in the Civil War?

A: On June 27, 1861, Commander James H. Ward of the USS *Thomas Freeborn* became the first U.S. naval officer killed in the war, as his warship and the USS *Reliance* attacked Confederate positions at Aquia Creek on the Potomac River.

Q: Who was the first officer to hold the rank of vice admiral in the U.S. Navy?

A: David G. Farragut was promoted to vice admiral on December 23, 1864, in honor of his capture of New Orleans and Mobile.

Q: What Union admiral amassed the largest amount of "prize money" from captured blockade runners during the war?

A: Naval officers and seamen of the Federal blockading were awarded part of the profits of captured blockade runners and Union Admiral Samuel P. Lee reaped $109,689 in prize money— making him the U.S. Navy's biggest wartime winner.

Q: How many ships were captured, burned, or sunk by the Confederate raider *Alabama*?

A: Between her launching in England in May 1862 and her sinking in June 1864, the *Alabama* captured, sank, or burned 69 ships.

Q: What was the difference between the Civil War-era warships *Merrimac* and *Merrimack*?

A: The USS *Merrimack* was a U.S. frigate launched in 1855, set afire by retreating Federal forces at Norfolk Navy Yard in 1861, and rebuilt as the Confederate ironclad CSS *Virginia*. The USS *Merrimac* was a Union sidewheel steamer commissioned in the summer of 1864.

Q: What was the only Federal warship sunk by the powerful Confederate ironclad CSS *Albemarle*?

A: On April 19, 1864, near Plymouth, North Carolina, the *Albemarle* rammed and sank the USS *Smithfield*—the only Union ship to be sunk by the famous Confederate ironclad.

Q: Where was headquarters for the U.S. West Gulf Squadron?
A: Pensacola, Florida.

Q: Where did Union Rear Admiral John Dahlgren lose his flagship in 1865?

A: Dahlgren, who was commander of the South Atlantic Blockading Squadron at war's end, lost his flagship, the USS *Harvest Moon*, in Winyah Bay, near Georgetown, South Carolina, when the ship struck a homemade Confederate torpedo on March 1, 1865.

Q: Besides designing the Union ironclad *Monitor*, what other important naval development was engineered by Swedish inventor John Ericsson?

A: The screw propeller.

Q: What unique post in the Confederate States Navy was held by Lieutenant William H. Parker?

A: Formerly a U.S. naval officer and instructor at the U.S. Naval Academy, Parker was chosen by Confederate Navy Secretary Stephen R. Mallory to serve as the first commandant of the Confederate States Naval Academy, which was established in 1863.

Q: What artificial adornment was worn by Gideon Welles, the Union secretary of the navy?

A: Welles wore a wig.

Q: What high-ranking Confederate naval officer had commanded the flagship during Commodore Matthew Perry's 1853 expedition to Japan, which opened that country to Western commerce?

A: Perry's flagship commander was Franklin Buchanan, who later commanded the CSS *Virginia* in its historic battle with the *Monitor*.

Q: What ship's sinking cost more lives than did the loss of any other vessel during the war?

A: On April 27, 1865, the Union steamer *Sultana*, overloaded with a cargo of mules and newly freed Union prisoners of war, blew up and sank on the Mississippi with a loss of more than 1,500 dead.

FACT: In 1864, a Confederate cavalry action destroyed three Union warships and captured two others. Near Alexandria, Louisiana, in May 1864, Confederate General James P. Major and a force of cavalry captured and destroyed the Federal tinclads *Signal* and *Covington* and the transport *Emma*, and also captured the transports *City Belle* and *Warner*.

Q: Who guarded the gold and silver bullion of the Confederate States Treasury when it was moved from Richmond during the city's fall in April 1865?

A: The Confederate Treasury's specie and bullion was moved by railroad and wagon from Richmond to Abbeville, South Carolina, where it was turned over to officials fleeing south with President Jefferson Davis. On the long route from Richmond to Abbeville the Confederate treasure was guarded by members of the cadet corps of the Confederate States Naval Academy.

(National Archives)

Q: Where was the Confederate commerce raider CSS *Florida* captured and what Union warship claimed her as a prize?

A: The CSS *Florida*, which captured more than 30 U.S. merchant ships, was captured off Bahia, Brazil, on October 7, 1864, by the USS *Wachusett*, which violated international law by seizing the raider in Brazilian waters. In the rare photograph above, the *Florida* makes a refueling stop at Funchal, Madeira, early in 1864.

Q: When the U.S. Navy's daily whiskey ration was outlawed by Congress midway through the war, what did the U.S. Navy's Bureau of Medical Surgery recommend as a substitute?

A: Oatmeal and water or iced coffee.

Q: What Confederate commerce raider was captured at Portland, Maine?

A: On June 26, 1863, after seizing a Federal revenue cutter, the Confederate schooner *Archer* was captured by Union naval forces; however, the Federals failed to capture the *Archer's* commander, Lieutenant Charles W. Reed, who had used his ship and another to capture 21 Northern vessels in 19 days.

Q: What Union admiral celebrated his birthday each year by turning a handspring—even at age 61?

A: The annual acrobatics were performed by Admiral David G. Farragut, who captured both New Orleans and Mobile during the war.

Q: The presence of what ceremonial gift for Confederate President Jefferson Davis almost led to the capture of the blockade runner *Banshee II*?

A: As the *Banshee II* quietly approached the entrance to Wilmington, North Carolina, late in the war, Union blockaders lying nearby were alerted by the neighing of a horse sent to President Davis from the government of Egypt aboard the *Banshee II*—which barely escaped capture.

Q: What prominent Northern admiral was the son of a Swedish diplomat?

A: Rear Admiral John A. Dahlgren, who commanded the South Atlantic Blockading Squadron during much of the war, was the son of the Swedish consul stationed in Philadelphia at the beginning of the nineteenth century.

Q: What Union monitor was sunk at the Battle of Mobile Bay?

A: On August 5, 1864, during the Union naval attack at Mobile Bay, the monitor *Tecumseh* hit a Confederate "torpedo" sea mine, which exploded and sank the *Tecumseh* with 93 crewmen aboard.

Q: What other Southern navy yard was destroyed by retreating Confederate forces on the same day Southern troops evacuated and destroyed Norfolk Navy Yard?

A: On May 10, 1862, withdrawing Confederate forces destroyed both the Norfolk and the Pensacola navy yards to prevent their use by the enemy.

Q: What happened to the guns aboard the Union ironclad *Keokuk*, which sank off the coast of Charleston, South Carolina, on April 8, 1863?

A: Working at night, the Confederate defenders of Charleston removed the *Keokuk*'s turret underwater and salvaged its guns for use in the defense of Charleston.

Q: What Confederate gunboat was built at Mars Bluff Navy Yard near Florence, South Carolina?

A: Named for the river on which it was constructed, the CSS *Pee Dee*, a twin-screw gunboat, was the only gunboat built at Mars Bluff Navy Yard. It was completed at war's end, just in time to be scuttled by its crew.

Q: Where were the refueling stations for the Union's South Atlantic and North Atlantic Blockading Squadrons?

A: Beaufort, South Carolina, was the refueling station for the South Atlantic Blockading Squadron and Beaufort, North Carolina, was the port where ships of the North Atlantic Blockading Squadron refueled.

Q: Who was appointed commandant of the newly organized Confederate States Marine Corps in 1861?

A: Colonel Lloyd J. Bell.

FACT: The first ship to raise the Confederate flag on the high seas was the CSS *Huntress*, a former mail packet bought in New York City by the state of Georgia in March 1861 and shortly afterward relinquished to the fledgling Confederate navy for duty out of Charleston.

Q: Who was the last commanding officer on the Union ironclad *Monitor*?

A: Commander John P. Bankhead, a veteran officer active in naval service throughout the war, was the commanding officer of the *Monitor* at the time the famous ship foundered and sank in a storm off Cape Hatteras on December 31, 1862.

Q: What kind of guns did the Confederate ironclad *Virginia* carry?

A: The CSS *Virginia* mounted six 9-inch smoothbore Dahlgrens, and four 6-inch and 7-inch rifled cannon.

Q: What kind of guns were mounted on the Union ironclad *Monitor*?

A: Two 11-inch smoothbore Dahlgrens.

Q: What did these Union ships have in common: the USS *Wabash*, the USS *Memphis*, and the USS *New Ironsides*?

A: All were attacked by the torpedo boat *David* while on blockade duty off the South Carolina coast.

Q: What was special about a Confederate dispatch boat named the *America*, which sank off the coast of South Carolina in 1862?

A: The dispatch boat was the famous yacht *America*, which had won the America's Cup from the British Royal Yacht Squadron in 1851. It was later raised and repaired by the U.S. Navy and in 1870 successfully defended its cup.

Q: What was the first Confederate commerce raider to operate against Northern shipping on the high seas?

A: The CSS *Sumter* was first, putting to sea under Captain Raphael Semmes on June 30, 1861.

Q: What U.S. gunboat made a dramatic dash past Confederate batteries at Island No. 10 on April 4, 1862, undermining the Confederate defenses on the Mississippi?

A: The USS *Carondelet*.

Q: Who was commander of the USS *Star of the West* when the ship was fired on attempting to supply Fort Sumter on January 9, 1861?

A: Captain John F. McGowan.

Q: What Northern admiral assumed an important Civil War command because his foster brother was too ill to accept it?

A: Admiral David D. Porter, above, commander of the U.S. Navy's Mississippi Squadron, was given command of the North Atlantic Blockading Squadron in September 1864, when his foster brother, Admiral David G. Farragut, declined the command because of poor health.

Q: Of the eight Confederate gunboats engaged against the nine-ship Union flotilla at the Battle of Memphis, how many Confederate vessels survived?

A: On June 6, 1862, Union Commodore Charles H. Davis led five U.S. ironclads and four rams with 68 guns against a makeshift Confederate squadron of eight vessels and 28 guns under Captain James E. Montgomery; at battle's end three Confederate ships were destroyed, four were captured, and only the CSS *Van Dorn* escaped.

Q: What Confederate ironclad ram was captured at the Battle of Mobile?

A: On August 5, 1864, Confederate Admiral Franklin Buchanan's flagship, the CSS *Tennessee*, was captured at the Battle of Mobile.

Q: How thick were the sides of the famous Confederate ironclad CSS *Virginia*?

A: The *Virginia*'s sides were protected by 4 inches of iron and below that, 22 inches of wood.

Q: What was unusual about the Northern clipper ship *Jacob Bell*, which was captured and burned by the Confederate commerce raider CSS *Florida*?

A: The *Jacob Bell*, captured by the *Florida* on February 12, 1863, while returning from China, carried a cargo valued at more than $2 million.

Q: How many blockade runners were captured or destroyed by the Federal navy during the war?

A: According to U.S. Secretary of the Navy Gideon Welles, 1,504 blockade runners had been captured or destroyed by the U.S. Navy by war's end.

Q: What happened to Confederate Captain Raphael Semmes, commander of the CSS *Alabama*, after his famous cruiser was sunk by the USS *Kearsarge* off the coast of France?

A: Although most survivors of the *Alabama*'s crew were rescued by the *Kearsarge*, Semmes and 41 others were rescued by a British yacht, the *Deerhound*, and thus escaped to England.

Q: What two Confederate forts did Admiral David G. Farragut's fleet have to pass under fire to capture New Orleans on April 24, 1862?

A: Fort Jackson and Fort St. Philip.

Q: What happened to the Confederate ironclad ram CSS *Albemarle* after she was sunk by a Union torpedo boat on October 28, 1864, near Plymouth, North Carolina?

A: The *Albemarle* was later raised by Union forces and at war's end was towed to Norfolk Navy Yard where it was condemned as a prize of war, bought by the U.S. Navy, then sold in 1867.

Q: What position was held at age 23 by Gideon Welles, the Union secretary of the navy during the war?

A: After graduating from college and studying law, Welles became editor of the *Hartford Times* of Connecticut—a post he held from 1827 to 1835, even while serving in the legislature.

Q: What eventually happened to the blockade runner *Colonel Lamb*, which was one of the Confederate navy's most successful commerce vessels?

A: Named for the commander of North Carolina's Fort Fisher, Colonel William Lamb, the *Colonel Lamb* made many successful runs through the Union blockade. Sold to the Greek government at war's end, it was renamed the *Bouboulina* and was accidentally blown up while taking on a cargo of explosives at Liverpool in 1867.

Q: When the Civil War began, the U.S. Navy had 90 ships, 1,300 officers, and 7,500 seamen. How large was the Union navy when the war ended?

A: At war's end in 1865, the U.S. Navy had swelled to 670 ships, 6,700 officers, and 51,500 seamen.

FACT: The last Confederate ironclad to surrender to Union forces in home waters was the CSS *Missouri*, which surrendered to the U.S. Navy at Shreveport, Louisiana, on June 3, 1865.

Q: What Confederate ship was commandeered by a slave crew and turned over to the U.S. Navy?

A: On May 12, 1862, Robert Smalls, a slave serving as a pilot aboard the armed dispatch and transport vessel *Planter*, took the ship from Charleston harbor while all officers were ashore, steamed into the Atlantic, raised a white flag, and surrendered the *Planter* with its slave crew to the USS *Onward*.

Q: How much had the U.S. Navy cost taxpayers by the end of the war?

A: The U.S. Navy, which began the war with an annual expenditure of $12 million, recorded an annual expenditure of $123 million in 1865.

(Library of Congress)

Q: What was the first Union warship sunk by a Confederate torpedo?

A: On December 12, 1862, the USS *Cairo*, above, struck a homemade Confederate mine, or torpedo, in Mississippi's Yazoo River and sank in 12 minutes—the first Union ship to be sunk by a Confederate torpedo in the Civil War.

Q: What eventually happened to the Confederate cruiser CSS *Sumter?*

A: After a six-month career as a commerce raider in which it captured 18 prizes, the *Sumter* was disarmed and sold at public auction in Gibraltar, was converted to the blockade runner *Gibraltar*, and remained an active commerce vessel until it reportedly sank in a storm off the coast of France in 1867.

Q: Who was the last survivor of the crew of the famous Union *Monitor?*

A: Thomas L. Taylor, a crewman at the time of the *Monitor's* sinking off the North Carolina coast on December 31, 1862, was the last *Monitor* crewman to die and is buried in Putnam, Connecticut.

Q: When Admiral Samuel F. Du Pont attacked Fort Sumter with nine Union ironclads on April 7, 1863, what ship was serving as Du Pont's flagship?

A: The USS *New Ironsides.*

Q: How did the commander of the Union ironclad *Monitor* send visual signals to other vessels in daytime?

A: The *Monitor* had no mast on which to hoist the official naval code, so messages were written in chalk on a blackboard, which was held up by a crewman to be viewed by other ships.

Q: What was the final fate of the Confederate raider *Florida?*

A: After its capture off the coast of Brazil in 1864, the *Florida* was brought to the U.S. naval station at Hampton Roads, where it was sunk.

8 | ARMS AND EQUIPMENT

Q: How many messages were sent daily by the Federal Military Telegraph System during the war?

A: The Military Telegraph System, directed by U.S. Secretary of War Edwin M. Stanton—a former director of the Atlantic and Ohio Telegraph Company—used 15,000 miles of wire during the war and sent approximately 3,300 coded messages per day.

Q: What were "shoddies"?

A: At the beginning of the war, Northern clothing contractors supplied the Union army with shoddily made uniforms that were manufactured from wool scraps. The uniforms fell apart on the march and in heavy rains, leading Union troops to call them "shoddies."

Q: Where was Scovill Manufacturing Company, the large Northern button manufacturer, whose backmark was stamped on millions of Union army buttons?

A: Scovill Manufacturing Company was located in Waterbury, Connecticut.

146

Q: What was the largest cannon in use during the Civil War?
A: The war's largest cannon was a 20-inch smoothbore gun designed by Thomas J. Rodman and cast at Fort Pitt in Pittsburgh. The giant cannon weighed 117,000 pounds and used 125 pounds of powder to fire a projectile weighing 1,080 pounds. It was mounted at Fort Hamilton, New York, and was fired in practice only four times during the war.

Q: What was "chuck-or-luck"?
A: It was a dice game played extensively by Civil War soldiers.

(U.S. Military Academy)

Q: Who invented the Armstrong rifled cannon used by some Confederate artillery units during the war?
A: Designed by British inventor Sir William Armstrong, the Armstrong rifled cannon was imported into the Confederacy through the blockade. Armstrong manufactured both field pieces and heavy artillery, like this 8-inch, 150-pounder Armstrong cannon captured by Union forces at Fort Fisher and put on display at West Point.

Q: Why was the Model 1855 Colt repeating rifle unpopular with Federal troops?

A: Samuel Colt's 1855 repeater, modeled after his famous six-shot pistol, sometimes leaked flame when fired and discharged all six barrels simultaneously, causing soldiers to mistrust the weapon.

Q: What were the Fort Sumter and Fort Pickens medals and who awarded them?

A: The bronze medals were struck in 1861 to be awarded Union veterans of the attacks on Fort Sumter in Charleston and Fort Pickens in Pensacola. They were produced and awarded by the New York City Chamber of Commerce.

Q: Who invented the Spencer repeating carbine?

A: The weapon was designed by arms inventor Christopher Spencer of Connecticut, who received a patent for the breechloader in 1860. By 1864 Union cavalry forces were routinely issued Spencer carbines.

Q: What were the differences in the three types of Civil War flags: a color, a standard, and an ensign?

A: A color was a flag carried by dismounted troops; a standard was carried by mounted units; and an ensign was flown from a ship.

Q: Who developed the Columbiad cannon?

A: The Columbiad was produced in 1811 by Colonel George Bomford of the U.S. Army and was used in the War of 1812.

Q: What was a "sap-roller"?

A: A "sap-roller" was a large, round basketlike roller made of bound brush and rolled by troops at the head of a trench to protect diggers when they were extending the approach to a besieged enemy position.

FACT: The famous Civil War minié ball was not a ball at all. It was a conical lead projectile with a hollow base that expanded when the bullet was fired, forcing the sides of the projectile to grip the riflings in the gun barrel and giving the bullet a spin that increased accuracy.

Q: What color was the lining of J. E. B. Stuart's cape and what kind of feather did he wear in his hat?

A: The flamboyant Stuart wore a red-lined cape and an ostrich plume.

Q: What food was regularly issued to Union soldiers in an attempt to prevent scurvy?

A: Dried potato slabs heavily seasoned with pepper and called "desiccated potatoes" were issued to Federal troops in the mistaken notion that they prevented scurvy. Most soldiers declined to eat the substance, claiming it produced a soup which resembled "a dirty brook with dead leaves floating around."

Q: What was the "Dictator"?

A: During the Siege of Petersburg, Union forces bombarded the Confederate lines with a 17,000-pound, 13-inch seacoast mortar, which Federal troops called the "Dictator" or the "Petersburg Express."

Q: What kind of weapon was manufactured for the Confederacy by a firm called the Nashville Plow Works?

A: Cavalry sabers.

Q: Where was the Palmetto Armory located?

A: The Palmetto Armory, a prewar musket manufacturer, produced ammunition and small arms for the Confederacy during the war and was located in Columbia, South Carolina.

Q: For whom was the Civil War's Coehorn Mortar named?

A: Baron Menno van Coehorn, a seventeenth-century Dutchman, invented the portable smoothbore mortar which bears his name.

Q: What was the Confederate motto placed on the officers' china used by the Confederate navy?

A: The motto was "Aide-toi et Dieu t'aidera"—"God helps those who help themselves."

Q: What was the standard artillery piece of the Civil War?

A: Although rifled cannon saw increased use in the war, the standard artillery piece used by both sides was the 12-pounder smoothbore Napoleon, adopted as standard by the U.S. Army in 1857.

Q: What were the principal foundries for casting cannon in the Confederacy?

A: The Tredegar Iron Works in Richmond was the Confederacy's main foundry and was the main producer of artillery for the South. The only other first-class foundry in the Confederacy was Leed's Foundry in New Orleans, which was forced to cease production of artillery when New Orleans fell to Federal forces in 1862.

Q: What kind of cartridges were used in the Sharps carbine?

A: Although metallic cartridges were used in the weapon after the Civil War, the wartime cartridges were linen or paper.

Q: What was canister?

A: Canister was a type of artillery ammunition which consisted of cylindrical tin cases—canisters—filled with cast-iron balls packed in sawdust. Fired at troops from a distance of 100 to 200 yards, it transformed the cannon into huge shotguns.

Q: Confederate uniform buttons stamped "A.V.C." represented what military unit?

A: The initials "A.V.C." stood for "Alabama Volunteer Corps."

Q: Who invented the Whitworth rifled cannon?

A: The innovative Whitworth cannon used with success by a handful of Confederate troops was invented in 1862 by English mechanical engineer Sir Joseph Whitworth, who later became a Congregationalist minister.

Q: What Civil War weapon was called "Old Wristbreaker"?

A: The heavy Model 1840 cavalry saber was dubbed "Old Wristbreaker" by the soldiers forced to use it.

FACT: According to Union surgeons' reports, less than 4 percent of all Civil War battle wounds were caused by bayonets or swords. Approximately 5 percent of reported wounds were made by artillery fire. More than 90 percent were caused by bullets.

Q: How were Federal ambulances equipped?

A: By 1863, each ambulance in the Army of the Potomac was equipped with two leather-covered benches, two kegs of water, a supply of beef broth, ample bandages, and two stretchers. Despite the array of life-saving devices, Federal soldiers persisted in calling ambulances "dead carts."

Q: With what type of rifle were Berdan's Sharpshooters equipped?

A: The Sharpshooters chose to equip themselves with the single-shot breech-loading 1859 Sharps rifle.

(Library of Congress)

Q: **What standard U.S. Army equipment was patterned after a device used by American Indians?**

A: The Sibley tent, like those above, was one of the standard shelters for Federal troops in the Civil War. It was invented prior to the war by Henry Hopkins Sibley, who became a Confederate general. As a U.S. Army officer stationed in the American West before the war, Sibley reportedly got the idea for the tent from the Indian tepees he had seen on the Plains.

Q: When the U.S. government abandoned the Harper's Ferry Arsenal and Armory, where did the Confederates move the captured equipment?

A: The machinery used in production of the Model 1855 U.S. rifle musket at Harper's Ferry was moved to the Richmond Armory and Arsenal, and the production equipment for the Model 1841 U.S. rifle was moved to the former U.S. arsenal in Fayetteville, North Carolina.

Q: Who invented the Brooke rifled cannon used by the Confederacy?

A: The Brooke gun, which looked much like the Parrot rifled cannon, was invented by Confederate Chief of Ordnance John M. Brooke of Florida, who also designed the armor and artillery aboard the Confederate ironclad CSS *Virginia.*

Q: How thick did Confederate engineers build the walls of earthen fortifications in order to withstand the bombardment of naval artillery?

A: Sixteen feet.

Q: When Civil War soldiers referred to "lampposts" in flight, what were they describing?

A: Artillery shells in flight could be seen as a long blur with the naked eye and took the appearance of flying lampposts.

Q: Why was the Model 1841 rifle, used by both sides in the war, called the "Mississippi Rifle"?

A: The "Mississippi Rifle," the first percussion rifle issued to U.S. troops, was so named because it was used by Jefferson Davis' 1st Mississippi Regiment at the end of the Mexican War.

Q: What was a "belly band," worn by some Civil War soldiers?

A: It was a flannel bandage mistakenly thought to relieve dysentery.

Q: For what military invention did the U.S. Patent Office issue patent number 36,836 on November 4, 1862?

A: Inventor Richard Gatling was issued this patent number for his rapid-fire weapon, the Gatling Gun, which gave him international fame, but was perfected and produced too late to be of service in the Civil War.

Q: What were *chevaux-de-frise?*
A: Logs fixed with sharpened spikes were called *chevaux-de-frise* and were used to protect defensive positions.

Q: What high-ranking Union official described the breech-loading rapid-fire rifles available to the U.S. Army as "newfangled gimcracks"?
A: Using these words, U.S. Chief of Ordnance James W. Ripley dismissed the breechloader and opposed its use for most of the war.

Q: What was produced for the Confederacy by the Memphis Novelty Works?
A: Established by Thomas S. Leech and Charles H. Rigdon, the Memphis Novelty Works produced swords, spurs, and military accoutrements for the Confederacy until the capture of Memphis by Federal forces.

Q: What was the standard metal used in the production of field artillery during the Civil War?
A: Bronze was adopted as the standard metal for U.S. field pieces in 1841, but when rifled cannon were introduced shortly before the war, wrought iron replaced bronze because wrought-iron riflings could take more stress.

Q: What was the "new model" army pistol?
A: The Model 1860 Colt revolver, the standard U.S. Army pistol of the war, was known by this name, and the earlier Model 1848 Colt revolver was called the "old model" army pistol.

FACT: The largest manufacturer of revolvers in the Confederacy was the firm of Griswold and Gunnison, which was established by Samuel Griswold and A. W. Gunnison in an old cotton-gin factory in Griswoldville, Georgia, in 1862. It produced more than 3,000 brass-framed copies of the .36-caliber U.S. Navy Colt before the factory was destroyed by Union troops in 1864.

Q: What was the *Intrepid?*

A: The *Intrepid,* above, was one of the Federal observation balloons used by "Professor" Thaddeus Lowe to make aerial reconnaissance of Confederate positions during the 1862 Peninsula Campaign. Using telegraph lines, Lowe provided the first aerial direction of artillery fire.

Q: When a Civil War soldier "wormed" a bullet, what was he doing?

A: To unload an unfired bullet from a muzzle-loading rifle, a soldier would attach a screw-type device called a "worm" to his rifle ramrod, insert it down the gun barrel, screw it into the soft lead, and then remove the projectile—a practice called "worming a bullet."

Q: Who invented the Watercap time fuse used by the U.S. Navy during the Civil War?

A: This brass fuse was used by the U.S. Navy in great quantities during the war and was developed by Cyrus Alger of the South Boston Foundry prior to the war.

Q: Who initiated the use of land mines in the Civil War?

A: In 1862, Confederate General Gabriel J. Rains, who experimented with explosives as a hobby, ordered live artillery shells with detonating devices buried near Yorktown, Virginia—the first use of explosive land mines in the Civil War.

Q: What major arms foundry was located near West Point, New York?

A: Cold Spring Foundry was located on the Hudson River opposite the U.S. Military Academy at West Point, and produced up to 7,000 artillery projectiles a week during wartime.

Q: What U.S. senator invented an artillery projectile and was killed when a sample of his work exploded?

A: Senator Charles T. James of Rhode Island, a major general of militia, invented the James artillery projectile used in the war and was killed when one of his projectiles exploded during a demonstration in New York in 1862.

Q: Who invented the 15-shot Henry repeating rifle, used effectively by some Union troops?

A: The revolutionary weapon was invented in 1860 by Tyler Henry, the plant superintendent of Winchester's New Haven Arms Company in Connecticut. Confederates referred to the weapon as "that Yankee rifle that can be loaded on Sunday and fired all week."

Q: How did the U.S. Army's XV Corps develop its distinctive cartridge-box corps badge?

A: Soon after the army corps in the war's Eastern theater began adopting corps badges, a veteran soldier of the XV Corps, which did not have a badge, encountered troops of the XII Corps wearing their new corps badge. When asked why the XV Corps did not have a badge, the battle-tested veteran slapped his cartridge box and said that the XV Corps' badge was "40 rounds in the cartridge box and 20 in the pocket"—a comment which resulted in the adoption of the cartridge-box symbol as the badge of the XV Corps.

Q: What were "Joe Brown's Pikes"?

A: To meet the shortage of weapons in the South, Governor Joseph E. Brown of Georgia ordered the production of several thousand iron-tipped pikes for arming Georgia troops, and the useless weapons became known by this name.

Q: What was the official name for hardtack?

A: The common hardtack cracker issued to Federal soldiers was made of flour and water and was officially designated "hard bread." The crackers were prone to spoilage, however, and were commonly called "worm castles" by Union troops.

Q: What was a havelock and how was it used?

A: A havelock was a white linen covering for a kepi—the type of cap worn by many Civil War soldiers—and it usually included a small cape which protected the soldier's neck from sunburn. It was modeled on the English havelock used by British troops in India.

Q: How many troops per year could be supplied with small arms by the Springfield Armory in Springfield, Massachusetts?

A: Approximately 250,000.

Q: What was the most popular food sold by Union sutlers in the Civil War?

A: Molasses cookies, which were sold at six for a quarter, were the most popular goods on the sutlers' shelves.

Q: What was the second most popular pistol of the war?

A: Next to the Model 1860 Colt revolver, the .44-caliber Remington revolver was the most popular handgun of the war.

Q: How much did the standard Union soldier's uniform weigh?

A: The all-wool Union blouse, trousers, and undershirt—minus all accoutrements—weighed six pounds and caused discomfort during Southern summer heat.

Q: What was an "infernal machine"?

A: This name was used to specify any type of explosive device which was designed for use in a surprise manner. The sea mines called "torpedoes," artillery shells used as land mines, and bombs disguised as coal were all types of "infernal machines."

Q: What was the primary anesthetic used by Civil War surgeons?

A: Although many Civil War surgeons considered anesthetics too dangerous for use, those who used them in the field or hospital usually chose chloroform.

Q: What was a "Confederate candle"?

A: When wartime shortages in the South depleted the wax candles common during the era, resourceful civilians and soldiers produced substitutes of beeswax and rosin, which were dubbed "Confederate candles."

Q: What was the occupation of Edward Maynard, who invented the Maynard carbine issued to many U.S. troops?

A: He was a dentist in Washington, D.C.

FACT: The common leather cartridge box issued routinely to Union infantrymen weighed four pounds when fully loaded. It was usually worn on the hip, attached to a wide leather breast belt. When worn on a waist belt, according to army physicians, the compact cartridge box often caused its wearer to suffer a hernia "caused by the pressure of the belt on the abdomen in marching and other laborious efforts."

Q: What was "buck and ball"?

A: Troops equipped with the old-model .69-caliber smoothbore musket were often issued "buck and ball" ammunition—a .69-caliber musket ball packed in a paper cartridge with three buckshot loaded on top of the ball.

Q: What was the difference between an artillery shot and an artillery shell?

A: A shot was a solid artillery projectile, while a shell was hollow and was loaded with black powder, which was ignited by a fuse to cause the shell to explode in deadly fragments.

Q: What was the most common rifle used by Union and Confederate soldiers in the war?

A: The principal rifle of the Civil War was the U.S. rifle musket, commonly called the Springfield rifle, which was used on both sides. More than 1.5 million of the Model 1861 and Model 1863 Springfield were manufactured during the war.

Q: What were gabions?

A: Large round basketlike objects made of brush, left with open ends, and sometimes topped with sandbags, gabions were used to fortify Civil War earthworks.

Q: Who was Major T. L. Bayne and why was he important to the Confederacy?

A: Bayne was the head of the Confederacy's Bureau of Foreign Supplies, which was responsible for importing arms and equipment from Europe.

Q: What was a soldier's "housewife"?

A: A "housewife" was a small sewing kit commonly carried by soldiers of both sides during the war.

FACT: Instant coffee was first widely used in the American Civil War. Coffee mixed with cream and sugar was distributed in paste form to Union soldiers, who tried to dissolve it in hot water to make a cup of coffee.

Q: What was the Stonewall Jackson Medal and to whom was it awarded?

A: It was a two-inch medal bearing an image of Jackson and was struck and manufactured for presentation to members of the Stonewall Brigade. None were awarded, however, and they remained crated in a West Indies port at war's end.

Q: What was the effective range of the 12-pounder smoothbore field piece, compared with the 12-pounder rifled gun?

A: The smoothbore gun had a maximum range of 1,400 yards but was most effective at 600 to 700 yards, while the rifled cannon had a maximum range of 1,800 yards and was most effective at 1,200 yards.

Q: Who invented the most common hand grenade of the Civil War?

A: William F. Ketchum of Buffalo, New York, invented the most familiar Civil War hand grenade—the Ketchum grenade—which saw limited use by Union troops.

Q: In an attempt to secure much-needed lead for the manufacture of bullets, Confederate Colonel George W. Rains organized a donation drive in Charleston, South Carolina, which produced more than 200,000 pounds of lead. What did he ask the citizens of Charleston to donate?

A: Lead window weights.

Q: What company produced the Burnside carbine?

A: The breech-loading Burnside was invented before the war by Union General Ambrose E. Burnside and was originally produced by his Bristol Firearms Company, which declared bankruptcy in 1860. Most of the 55,567 Burnside carbines bought by the Federal government during the war were manufactured by the Burnside Arms Company, which was owned by Burnside's creditors.

Q: Where was the Kerr revolver manufactured?

A: The .44-caliber, five-shot Kerr revolver used by some Confederate officers and cavalrymen was imported from England and was manufactured at the London Armory.

Q: Where was the Confederate button supplier Courtney & Tennet located?

A: In Charleston, South Carolina.

Q: What was the maximum range of a 15-inch Columbiad heavy artillery piece?

A: A little over two miles.

(Library of Congress)

Q: What were the "butternuts" commonly worn by Confederate troops?

A: When wartime shortages made gray uniforms unavailable, Confederate troops, like these soldiers captured at Gettysburg, attired themselves in uniforms dyed brown with walnut hulls or butternut bark—producing the famous "butternuts" worn as a substitute for Confederate gray.

Q: What weapon was produced at the Asheville Armory in Asheville, North Carolina?

A: The principal product of the Asheville Armory was a rough copy of the British Enfield rifle and was produced in limited numbers and marked "Asheville" on the lock plate.

Q: Where was rank insignia worn on the uniforms of Confederate and Union officers?

A: The rank of Union officers was indicated by shoulder straps or epaulettes, while the rank of Confederate officers was designated by collar insignia.

Q: Who invented the paper cartridge commonly used in small arms by both sides in the war?

A: King Gustavus Adolphus of Sweden.

Q: What were battle streamers, used by Federal regiments?

A: In 1862, the U.S. War Department ordered all units to attach battle streamers bearing the names of the battles in which the units had fought to the staffs of all the colors carried by the units.

Q: Who invented the Confederate Archer artillery projectile?

A: The Archer projectile, which saw limited use in the war, was invented by Dr. Junius Archer, owner of the Bellona Arsenal Foundry near Midlothian, Virginia.

Q: Who invented percussion caps?

A: The percussion cap, a small metal cap containing an explosive element, was used to fire rifles and pistols during the war, and was the invention of Alexander Forsyth, a Scottish minister.

Q: How many rounds of small-arms ammunition were produced by the Richmond Arsenal during the war?

A: From July 1, 1861, to January 1, 1865, more than 72 million rounds of small-arms ammunition was manufactured at the Richmond Arsenal.

Q: In the Union army, what did mess gear consist of?

A: By the end of 1863, standard mess gear issued to Union troops consisted of a spoon, a fork, a knife, and a tin plate.

Q: What state issued its troops brass uniform buttons adorned with a palmetto tree?

A: Troops in state service from South Carolina were issued buttons stamped with the state seal, which included a palmetto tree.

Q: How many men were in a Civil War regimental color guard?

A: Each regiment had a color guard of four carefully selected soldiers—two who carried the regimental colors and two who guarded them.

Q: What image was stamped on the shiny brass breastplates which adorned Union cartridge-box straps?

A: An eagle.

Q: How many artillery harnesses, saddles, and horseshoes were manufactured by the Confederate Armory in Augusta, Georgia, in 1863 and 1864?

A: During a two-year period at the height of the war, the Augusta plant produced 2,535 single sets of artillery harnesses, 2,455 saddles, and 73,521 horseshoes.

Q: What was the main source of ammunition for the Confederate Army of Tennessee?

A: The Atlanta Arsenal was the principal supplier of ammunition for the Army of Tennessee until Atlanta fell to Union forces in 1864.

Q: Who developed the Britten artillery projectile?

A: Englishman Bashley Britten invented and manufactured the Britten projectile, which was used primarily by Confederate artillery.

FACT: The imported British Enfield rifle so popular with Confederate soldiers was named for its source of manufacture—the British armory at Enfield, England. There the British government operated an armory almost identical to the American one at Springfield, Massachusetts.

Q: What was "salt horse"?

A: It was U.S. Army–issue salted beef, designed not to decay for up to two years and so saturated with salt preservative that soldiers had to soak it in water for hours prior to consumption.

Q: How many rounds of small-arms ammunition were produced by the U.S. Ordnance Department during the 1863 fiscal year?

A: Two hundred and fifty-nine million.

(Library of Congress)

Q: How much did a 13-inch Union seacoast mortar weigh?

A: Monster seacoast mortars, like these in a Union battery at Yorktown in 1862, could fire a projectile weighing up to 770 pounds and, with some shot, had a range of almost four-fifths of a mile. A 13-inch seacoast mortar weighed more than 17,000 pounds.

9 | ODDITIES OF THE WAR

Q: Who was the first soldier killed in the Civil War?

A: On April 14, 1861, a member of the Federal garrison at Fort Sumter, Private Daniel Hough of the 1st U.S. Artillery, was accidentally killed by an exploding cannon during evacuation ceremonies at Fort Sumter—making Hough the first combat soldier killed in the Civil War.

Q: At what battle did the lyrics of a song stop a Union retreat?

A: In May 1864, at the Battle of the Wilderness, the Union IX Corps was in danger of being turned by a strong Confederate attack when one of the soldiers in blue yelled out the opening words of "The Battle Cry of Freedom"—"We'll rally round the flag;/Boys, we'll rally once again!"—and the Northern troops held their ground.

Q: What food was Confederate General Stonewall Jackson known to consume in battle?

A: Jackson had a fondness for lemons and habitually sucked them— even in combat.

Q: How many pairs of gloves were owned by Mary Todd Lincoln while she was First Lady?

A: More than 300.

Q: What prominent Confederate cabinet officer became legal counsel to the queen of England after the Civil War?

A: Confederate Secretary of State Judah P. Benjamin, a former New Orleans attorney who had entered Yale University at age 14, fled through Florida to the Bahamas at war's end, then moved to England, where he became legal counsel to Queen Victoria in 1872.

(Library of Congress)

Q: What was the typical salary of a newspaper correspondent in the Civil War?

A: Standard pay for a top-rated reporter from a large daily newspaper was $25 a week plus expenses. Combat artists like Alfred R. Waud of *Harper's Weekly*, above, were not paid much better. Some correspondents allegedly made extra money on the sly by writing favorable stories about high-ranking officers.

Q: What Union officer received the Japanese Order of the Rising Sun?

A: Colonel Charles Le Gendre, a French-born commander of New York troops at New Berne and the Wilderness, became an adviser to the Japanese government after the war and was awarded the Second Class of Merit of the Order of the Rising Sun from the Japanese emperor.

Q: What family tragedies struck both Abraham Lincoln and Jefferson Davis during their presidencies?

A: Both lost sons while in office: Lincoln's 12-year-old Willie died of typhoid in 1862, and Davis' 5-year-old Joe died when he fell from a balcony in 1864.

Q: On November 21, 1864, Abraham Lincoln penned a famous letter of consolation to Mrs. Lydia Bixby, expressing sympathy for the death of five sons who "died gloriously on the field of battle." What was wrong with his letter?

A: When he wrote his eloquent message, consoling Mrs. Bixby for the death of five sons on "the altar of freedom," Lincoln did not know that only two sons had died—one was discharged and two were deserters.

Q: What was ironic about the location chosen for the funeral of Confederate General John Pegram, who was killed at age 33 in an engagement at Hatcher's Run, Virginia, on February 6, 1865?

A: Pegram's funeral was held in Richmond's St. Paul's Church, where he had been married only three weeks earlier.

FACT: The USS *Star of the West*, the famous supply ship which was fired on by Southern forces during the Siege of Fort Sumter in 1861, did not survive the war. Three months after being turned away from Fort Sumter by gunfire, the *Star of the West* was captured by Confederate forces at Indianola, Texas, and on March 13, 1863, was sunk in Mississippi's Tallahatchie River in an attempt to block the Union navy's approach to Vicksburg.

Q: What unusual postwar position was held by John Surratt, an accused member of the Lincoln assassination conspiracy?

A: The son of Mary E. Surratt, the boardinghouse operator hanged as a conspirator in the Lincoln assassination, John Surratt fled to Europe after Lincoln's murder and eventually became a member of the Papal Guard in Rome. The conspiracy charges against him were never proved.

Q: What Civil War document bore these names: George Hogtoter, Jumper Duck, Bone Eater, Spring Water, John Bearmeat, and Big Mush Dirt Eater?

A: All are names listed on the muster roll of the Indian Brigade, a force of Union troops recruited from the tribes of the Indian Territory, in what is now Oklahoma.

Q: Why was Ulysses S. Grant angered with *New York Times* correspondent William Swinton during the 1864 Wilderness Campaign?

A: During a nighttime war council between Grant, Meade, and other officers, Swinton was discovered hiding behind a stump, eavesdropping on the conference. He was later barred from the army.

Q: What two brothers became Civil War generals on opposite sides and were both killed in action?

A: Brigadier General William R. Terrill of Virginia, a West Point graduate and instructor, was a Union brigade commander at the time of his death at the Battle of Perryville in 1862. His younger brother, James B. Terrill, a graduate of VMI, was a Confederate brigadier general who was killed in action in 1864 at Bethesda Church.

Q: Where was Andrew Johnson administered the oath of office as president of the United States?

A: On April 15, 1865, Johnson was sworn in as president in his suite at the Kirkwood Hotel on 12th Street in Washington.

Q: What famous Old West lawman served as a Union scout at the Battle of Pea Ridge?

A: "Wild Bill" Hickock.

Q: What Civil War officer recorded the highest grades attained at West Point in the nineteenth century?

A: Confederate General William Henry Chase Whiting, who graduated at the top of his class at West Point in 1845, held the record for the highest grades ever attained at West Point—a record that lasted until a new one was established by Douglas MacArthur in 1903.

Q: What Confederate soldier assigned to General Nathan Bedford Forrest's command became an infamous figure of the Old West?

A: The notorious gunfighter Clay Allison, who was later blamed for a string of killings in Texas and New Mexico, served as a scout for Forrest during the last half of the war. Earlier he had been discharged from regular Confederate service because of "emotional instability."

Q: What Confederate general deserted from service and retired to Canada?

A: General Daniel M. Frost, a New York native appointed a Confederate general from Missouri, left the army without tendering his resignation in 1863 and sat out the rest of the war with his family in Canada.

Q: What Confederate soldier became a German field marshal in World War I?

A: Wounded at Dranesville, Virginia, in 1864, Baron Von Massow, a member of Colonel John S. Mosby's Partisan Rangers, later became chief of cavalry in the Imperial German Army and in World War I was field marshal and commander of the 9th German Army Corps.

FACT: On December 17, 1863, the U.S. Congress awarded the only gold medal given by the U.S. government to a soldier in the Civil War. It was awarded to General Ulysses S. Grant in appreciation for the capture of Vicksburg and Chattanooga by forces under his command.

Q: In what official capacity did women serve in the U.S. Army during
the Civil War?

A: Women were attached to the Union army as nurses, laundresses,
and stewardesses. Most were active primarily when troops were in
camp, although some nurses followed the soldiers to the front.
Some women, like this hard-working laundress with the 31st
Pennsylvania, somehow performed their duties while simultaneously
managing children and pets.

Q: What was assassin John Wilkes Booth's military experience?

A: Booth, who had chosen not to enter Confederate military service despite his Southern sympathies, had served in a Virginia militia unit which participated in the capture of John Brown at Harper's Ferry in 1859.

Q: Who was the oldest officer to leave the prewar U.S. Army for Confederate service?

A: General David E. Twiggs, who was 71 in 1862, was the oldest army officer to join the Confederacy, although he was not given a field command due to his age.

Q: What became of Robert E. Lee's headquarters records?

A: They were believed to have been destroyed when the 1st Pennsylvania Cavalry burned a Confederate wagon train near Amelia Springs, Virginia, during the Appomattox Campaign.

Q: What was the name of General George G. Meade's favorite horse?

A: Baldy, Meade's favorite mount, survived wounds at First Manassas, Antietam, and Gettysburg; carried Meade in action at Fredricksburg and Gettysburg; and trailed Meade's hearse at his funeral in 1872.

Q: What Confederate general was captured by U.S. forces, then was allowed an office in New York City by the U.S. government?

A: General William Beall of Kentucky was captured at Port Hudson but was later allowed to open a New York City office to provide supplies for Confederate prisoners and to work in prisoner exchange.

Q: How much was the reward offered by the U.S. War Department for the capture of Jefferson Davis at war's end?

A: One hundred thousand dollars in gold.

Q: Why did the *New York World* falsely report that Grant's 1864 offensive in Virginia had ended in defeat and failure?

A: The *World* was deceived by a hoax in which two reporters unsuccessfully tried to drive down gold prices and reap personal fortunes by planting false news of a major Union defeat.

Q: What Western town was named for Varina Davis, wife of the Confederate president?

A: According to local lore, the mining town of Virginia City, Montana, had been named Varina by its transplanted Southern residents. A Northern judge refused to record the name, but as a compromise officially listed the town as Virginia City.

Q: What two infamous outlaws of the Old West participated in the 1864 Centralia Massacre?

A: On September 27, 1864, Centralia, Missouri, was raided by a force of Confederate bushwhackers who robbed a train, killed civilian passengers, murdered unarmed Union soldiers, and virtually wiped out three companies of the U.S. 39th Missouri. Among the bushwhackers were two men who would later become perhaps the most notorious badmen of the Old West— Frank and Jesse James.

Q: How much did Abraham Lincoln's coffin cost?

A: For Lincoln's burial, the U.S. commissioner of public buildings purchased from the undertakers Sands and Harvey of Washington a walnut coffin costing $1,500. The coffin was lined with lead and trimmed with silver mountings; its interior was lined with white satin and silk.

Q: What prominent White House figure tried to keep Lincoln from making his Gettysburg Address?

A: On the day Lincoln left for Gettysburg to deliver his speech, his ten-year-old son Tad was ill, and First Lady Mary Lincoln tried strenuously and unsuccessfully to persuade him to cancel his speech.

Q: Why was it said of Wilmer McLean that the Civil War began in his front yard and ended in his parlor?

A: The first major land battle of the war, First Bull Run, spilled onto the farm of Virginian Wilmer McLean, whose house was struck by artillery fire. To escape the fighting, McLean moved to southern Virginia and bought a farm at Appomattox Court House, but he was unable to avoid the war: Lee surrendered to Grant in McLean's parlor.

Q: How did Confederate General Joseph E. Johnston die?

A: Johnston, who surrendered his army to Union General William T. Sherman, died on March 21, 1891, from pneumonia, which he contracted while marching in the rain as a pallbearer at Sherman's funeral.

Q: What famous American figure was the grandfather of Confederate General George W. Randolph?

A: Thomas Jefferson.

Q: In June 1861, why did a *Confederate* general command the Army of the Potomac encamped in northern Virginia?

A: Because it was a Confederate army—the *Confederate* Army of the Potomac—which was commanded by General P. G. T. Beauregard and later by General Joseph E. Johnston before being renamed the Army of Northern Virginia by Robert E. Lee.

Q: What was odd about General Thomas F. Drayton's surrender of the Confederate defenses at Port Royal Sound on November 7, 1861?

A: General Drayton's brother, Percival Drayton, a Union naval officer, commanded one of the warships which bombarded General Drayton's defenses into submission.

Q: Who was the only Confederate general to commit suicide during the Civil War?

A: Brigadier General Philip St. George Cocke of Virginia, a West Point graduate and a brigade commander at First Bull Run, returned to his home in poor health a few months after the battle and committed suicide the day after Christmas 1861.

FACT: Because of his controversial rule as military governor of New Orleans, Union General Benjamin F. Butler was ordered shot on sight by Confederate President Jefferson Davis. Ironically, Butler—a prominent Democrat—had disrupted the 1860 Democratic convention by voting 57 times for his favorite presidential candidate: U.S. Senator Jefferson Davis.

Q: What was odd about William Cain, a drillmaster of new recruits in the 25th North Carolina?

A: He was a 13-year-old cadet drillmaster from Hillsborough Military Academy.

Q: What was the twentieth-century occupation of Freeman Gosden, the son of Walter W. Gosden, who was a soldier in Mosby's Rangers?

A: Gosden, whose father rode with the famous "Rebel Raider," Colonel John Singleton Mosby, became "Amos" on the "Amos 'n' Andy" radio program.

(Library of Congress)

Q: What were "Sherman's hairpins"?

A: During their devastating march across Georgia, troops in General William T. Sherman's Union army, like these soldiers at Atlanta, destroyed railway lines by pulling up the iron railroad rails, heating them red-hot on fires, then twisting them into U-shapes which they jokingly called "Sherman's hairpins."

Q: Who wrote the Confederate marching song "The Bonnie Blue Flag"?

A: Harry Macarthy, a New Orleans comedian and songwriter, wrote the lyrics to the song in 1861, using an old Irish tune called "The Jaunting Car."

Q: What Civil War singing group was officially banned from performing before the Union Army of the Potomac?

A: The Hutchinson Family Singers of New Hampshire, popular performers of abolitionist songs, were forbidden to sing in army camps by Commanding General George B. McClellan after troops in the Army of the Potomac protested the antislavery tunes. President Lincoln later rescinded the order.

Q: Where was Confederate General Albert Sidney Johnston's surgeon when Johnston bled to death from a leg wound at Shiloh?

A: Johnston had sent his surgeon, Dr. D. W. Yandell, to the rear to treat wounded Union captives.

Q: What prominent Northern publisher helped post bail for Jefferson Davis when the Confederate president was imprisoned at war's end?

A: Republican newspaper editor Horace Greeley, founder of the *New York Tribune* and an ardent abolitionist, helped Davis post the bail necessary to be released by U.S. authorities—an act which prompted many *Tribune* readers to cancel their subscriptions.

Q: How did President Andrew Johnson learn to read?
A: His wife taught him shortly after they were married.

Q: Thirteen of the 16 officers in the 2d Massachusetts who were killed in the war were alumni of what college?
A: Harvard.

Q: What other tragedy struck Ford's Theater?
A: In 1893, after the government confiscated the theater and converted it to an office building, the building collapsed, killing 28 government employees.

Q: Who was the only American Indian to become a general in Confederate service?

A: Stand Watie, a Cherokee Indian leader, raised troops among the minority of Cherokees in present-day Oklahoma who sided with the Confederacy, saw action at Wilson's Creek and Pea Ridge, and was promoted to brigadier general in 1864.

Q: What Confederate general died because of a broken stirrup?

A: Brigadier General William E. Baldwin, a South Carolinian who was captured at Fort Donelson in 1862 and at Vicksburg in 1863, was killed in 1864 near Mobile, Alabama, when a broken stirrup caused him to fall from his horse.

Q: What Federal general was declared killed in action and was mistakenly "buried" while still alive?

A: At the Battle of Malvern Hill, on July 1, 1862, General Henry Barnum was left for dead on the battlefield. Another officer was mistakenly buried under Barnum's name and Barnum was counted as one of the dead—until he was discovered to be a prisoner of war.

Q: What Union general accepted the surrender of two major Southern armies in the Confederate capitulation of 1865?

A: Grant received the surrender of the Army of Northern Virginia; Sherman accepted the surrender of the Army of Tennessee; and General E. R. S. Canby received the surrender of two armies— the 12,000 troops of the Confederate Department of Alabama, Mississippi, and East Louisiana and the 43,000 troops of the Confederate Trans-Mississippi Department.

FACT: If Private Sam Blalock of the 26th North Carolina seemed to be an old friend of messmate Keith Blalock, it was understandable. "Sam" Blalock was really Malinda Blalock, wife of Private Keith Blalock. She had chosen to follow her husband into service and had successfully disguised her sex for months of camp, drill, and regimental duties.

Q: Was Robert E. Lee ever compensated for the seizure of his Arlington estate, which became Arlington National Cemetery?

A: Lee died without receiving any compensation for the loss of his property, but his heirs were eventually awarded compensation of $150,000 by the U.S. government.

Q: What Confederate general was killed in battle in Mexico four months after Appomattox?

A: General Mosby M. Parsons of Virginia, who fled to Mexico at war's end and joined Maximilian's army, was killed in an exchange of fire with Mexican partisans on August 15, 1865.

Q: Who was the last Confederate general to occupy a seat in the U.S. Congress?

A: General George Washington Gordon of Tennessee, a veteran of Stone's River, Chickamauga, Chattanooga, Atlanta, and Franklin, was a three-term U.S. congressman at the time of his death in 1911—the last former Confederate general in the U.S. Congress.

Q: What was unusual about the 1st through the 6th U.S. Volunteer Infantry?

A: These regiments, which fought Indians on the Western frontier in 1864–65, were composed of Confederate prisoners of war who had joined the U.S. Army to escape prison.

Q: What were the Dahlgren Papers and why were they controversial?

A: They were documents found on the body of Union Colonel Ulric Dahlgren, who was killed while on an unsuccessful cavalry raid against Richmond in 1864. The papers allegedly revealed Dahlgren's plans to kill Confederate President Jefferson Davis and his cabinet—a charge Dahlgren's defenders denied.

Q: Why was Confederate General Adam R. Johnson known as "Stovepipe"?

A: A leader of Confederate partisans in Kentucky, Johnson captured the town of Newburgh, Indiana, from a large garrison of Union troops by bluffing a surrender with 12 men and "artillery" made from an old wagon and joints of stovepipe—a feat which earned him the nickname "Stovepipe."

Q: What was unusual about the capture of Union City, Tennessee, by Nathan Bedford Forrest's Confederate forces on March 24, 1864?

A: Union City was surrendered to the Confederate 7th Tennessee Cavalry by the Union 7th Tennessee Cavalry.

Q: What Confederate general was paralyzed in a fall from a camel?

A: French-born General Raleigh E. Colston, a division commander under Stonewall Jackson at Chancellorsville, was a colonel in the Egyptian army after the war and was paralyzed when he fell from a camel while on an expedition in North Africa.

(Library of Congress)

Q: When and where did Civil War soldiers attend worship services?

A: Worship services for soldiers of the Civil War were usually scheduled on Sunday afternoons to avoid conflict with Sunday morning inspection. Services were held in tents or in hastily built chapels. Federal troops, like these New Yorkers, above, could receive canvas roofing, stoves, and hymnbooks from the North's Christian Commission if they agreed to build wooden walls for a chapel.

Q: What former West Point instructor left his post as street commissioner of New York City to become a general in the Confederate army?

A: Kentucky native Gustavus W. Smith, a civil engineer, left his job with the City of New York to accept a major general's commission in the Confederate army. He held a variety of wartime commands and after the war eventually returned to New York City.

Q: Why were the female onlookers from Maryland embarrassed to see Robert E. Lee's army crossing the Potomac River during Lee's 1863 invasion of the North?

A: The Maryland ladies, who had come to the Potomac to view Lee's army, were shocked to see the long columns of Confederate soldiers wading the river in their ragged underwear, with trousers and equipment held overhead.

Q: How long did it take Abraham Lincoln to deliver his famous Gettysburg Address?

A: Five minutes.

Q: How did Confederate General J. E. B. Stuart trick the opposing Union forces at the Battle of Second Manassas?

A: Stuart ordered some of his horsemen to drag brush along the dirt roads, stirring up huge clouds of dust which appeared to be large bodies of troops on the move. He thus convinced the opposing Federals that Confederate reinforcements were arriving.

Q: What Northern housewife received an official soldier's discharge after participating in the Battles of First Bull Run and New Berne?

A: Kady Brownell, African-born daughter of a British soldier, accompanied her husband Robert when he went into battle with Rhode Island troops at First Bull Run and New Berne. She eventually received a discharge from Major General Ambrose E. Burnside.

Q: What was the name of General George B. McClellan's favorite horse?

A: Daniel Webster.

Q: What famous Confederate general died of yellow fever with his wife and daughter?

A: General John Bell Hood, commander of the Army of Tennessee at Atlanta, Franklin, and Nashville, was a postwar businessman in New Orleans, where he and his wife and oldest daughter died of yellow fever in 1878.

Q: What was unusual about the prisoner of war captured by Union officer W. C. P. Breckinridge during the Battle of Atlanta?

A: The prisoner was Confederate J. C. Breckinridge—the brother of his captor.

Q: What Union general helped treat two assassinated U.S. presidents?

A: General Joseph K. Barnes, surgeon general of the United States at war's end, was present at Lincoln's deathbed and later attended President Garfield after he was shot by an assassin.

Q: What unusual postwar positions were held by Colonel William M. Dye of the 20th Iowa, who was decorated for actions at Vicksburg, during the Red River Campaign, and at Mobile?

A: After the war Dye served for a while in the Egyptian army and eventually became military adviser to the king of Korea.

Q: How much did First Lady Mary Todd Lincoln pay for the dress she wore to the 1865 inauguration?

A: Two thousand dollars.

FACT: Playwright William Shakespeare indirectly helped identify Lincoln assassin John Wilkes Booth. After Booth was shot and killed in a Virginia barn, U.S. officials wondered if they had gotten the right man—until the dead actor's body was identified by Dr. John F. May. A surgeon who had treated Booth, May identified the dead assassin by a scar on his neck. The actor had been scratched by an overly enthusiastic actress during an amorous embrace in a production of Shakespeare's *Romeo and Juliet*.

Q: What wartime emancipation plan proposed by Abraham Lincoln became a law—and failed?

A: On April 2, 1862—eight months before the famous Emancipation Proclamation became law—the U.S. Senate approved a House plan proposed by Lincoln which offered financial compensation to any state adopting gradual emancipation of slaves, but none of the Northern states where slaves were held adopted the provision.

Q: What two Confederate generals engaged in a fatal duel?

A: On September 6, 1863, at Little Rock, Arkansas, General John S. Marmaduke of Missouri and General Lucius M. Walker of Tennessee settled a dispute with a pistol duel—in which General Walker was shot to death.

Q: Who was William C. Quantrill's girlfriend and what did she do with the inheritance he left her?

A: When Colonel Quantrill, the notorious Confederate guerrilla leader, died from wounds in 1864, he left girlfriend Kate Clarke $500 in gold, with which she reportedly financed a brothel.

Q: Who was the only Confederate officer promoted from captain to general during the war?

A: General Victor Girardey, a captain of Georgia troops at the Battle of the Crater in 1864, so distinguished himself in the battle that he was promoted to brigadier general—only 13 days before he was killed in action near Richmond.

Q: Who were the only two foreign-born Confederate officers to rise to the rank of major general?

A: General Patrick R. Cleburne, an Irishman, and General Camille Armand Jules Marie, Prince de Polignac of France, were the only Confederate major generals born outside the United States.

Q: What Union officer was reportedly denied a promotion to general because nobody could pronounce his name?

A: Colonel Wladimir Krzyzanowski, a Polish immigrant who commanded New York troops, reportedly failed to get confirmation as general from the U.S. Senate because the lawmakers could not pronounce his name.

Q: What prominent role in the Appomattox surrender was played by a Seneca Indian?

A: The son of an Indian chief from New York, Lieutenant Colonel Ely Parker, Grant's military secretary, transcribed the official copies of terms of surrender at Appomattox.

Q: What Union naval officer was recruited into the U.S. Navy for his skills as a poet?

A: New England poet Henry Brownell published some poetry in the *Hartford Evening Post* which was admired by Union Admiral David G. Farragut. Soon afterward Farragut offered him an officer's commission in the U.S. Navy. Brownell spent much of the war as master's mate and secretary to Farragut.

Q: How did the first commander of the U.S. Army Signal Corps become interested in communications?

A: Major Albert J. Myer, the first commander of the U.S. Army Signal Corps, developed an interest in visual communications while experimenting with a language system for the hearing disabled during his days at medical school.

Q: What were the names of Robert E. Lee's famous horse before the mount was named Traveller?

A: Traveller was first named Jeff Davis, then Greenbrier, but by the time Lee rose to fame as the commander of the Army of Northern Virginia his famous gray horse was known as Traveller.

Q: Name the two Crittenden brothers who became generals.

A: Major General Thomas L. Crittenden, a Union general from Kentucky and the son of U.S. Senator John J. Crittenden, was the brother of George B. Crittenden, who was also a major general—in the Confederate army.

FACT: When young Abraham Lincoln enlisted in the 1832 Black Hawk War, the U.S. Army officer who accepted his enlistment was Lieutenant Robert Anderson—the officer who would accept President Lincoln's orders three decades later as the commander of besieged Fort Sumter.

Q: What member of Ulysses S. Grant's original staff was the last to die?

A: Colonel William S. Hillyer, a friend of Grant's before the war and his aide-de-camp during parts of the war, died in 1874—the last survivor from Grant's original Civil War staff.

Q: What prominent Confederate general had a son who became a lieutenant general in the U.S. Army in World War II?

A: Simon Bolivar Buckner of Kentucky, a lieutenant general in the Confederate army, had a son, Simon Bolivar Buckner, Jr., who became a lieutenant general in the U.S. Army and was killed on Okinawa in 1945.

(Library of Congress)

Q: What was the name of General Ulysses S. Grant's favorite horse?

A: Grant's favorite mount was named Cincinnati and was given to him in 1864. Other horses used by Grant during the war were Kangaroo, Fox, Jeff Davis, and Jack. Noted for his skills as an equestrian, Grant liked large, powerful horses. Above, he poses with Cincinnati.

Q: What was the assumed name of John Rowlands, a Confederate deserter who joined the Union navy—only to desert from that duty also?

A: Two-time deserter John Rowlands later adopted the alias "Henry M. Stanley," explored Africa, and reportedly uttered the famous query: "Dr. Livingstone, I presume?"

Q: For the capture of what Confederate general did the government of Spain offer a reward of $100,000?

A: In 1870, the Spanish government offered the reward for the capture of former Confederate General Thomas Jordan, a veteran of First Manassas, Shiloh, and Charleston, because Jordan had become the chief of staff of the Cuban revolutionary army.

Q: What Confederate general became a justice of the New York Supreme Court after the war?

A: General Roger A. Pryor of Virginia was present at the 1861 firing on Fort Sumter and led Confederate troops at the Seven Days' Battles, Second Manassas, and Antietam. At the end of the war he moved to New York City and eventually gained a seat on the New York Supreme Court.

Q: Who was the first general killed in the Civil War?

A: General Robert S. Garnett of Virginia, the first general to die in the war, was shot to death by Federal troops in a rearguard action near Corrick's Ford, Virginia, on July 13, 1861.

Q: What revival hymn originated with a message from General William T. Sherman?

A: The nineteenth-century gospel hymn "Hold the Fort" was based on a series of messages sent by Sherman to Union forces under attack at Allatoona, Georgia, in 1864. Actually, the main message, sent by signal flag, read, "General Sherman says hold fast. We are coming."

FACT: The tallest soldier on record in the Union army was Captain Charles Van Buskirk of the 27th Indiana Infantry. The captain's official height was recorded at 6'10½".

Q: What Confederate leader became the principal compiler of Confederate records for the massive *War of the Rebellion: The Official Records of the Union and Confederate Armies*, published by the U.S. government after the war?

A: General Marcus J. Wright, a Memphis attorney and a veteran of Shiloh, Perryville, and Chickamauga, spent almost 50 years after the war collecting Confederate records for the *War of the Rebellion* in an attempt to preserve an accurate chronicle of the war.

Q: When was the Confederate flag last officially lowered?

A: On November 6, 1865, Lieutenant James I. Waddell lowered the flag aboard the CSS *Shenandoah* at Liverpool, England—bringing down the Confederate colors officially for the last time.

BIBLIOGRAPHY

Adams, George W. *Doctors in Blue: The Medical History of the Civil War.* New York: Henry Shuman, 1952.

Albaugh, William, and Edward Simmons. *Confederate Arms.* Harrisburg: The Stackpole Company, 1957.

Albert, Alphaeus H. *Record of American Uniform and Historical Buttons.* Boyertown: Boyertown Publishing Company, 1976.

Alexander, Edward Porter. *Military Memoirs of a Confederate.* New York: Charles Scribner's Sons, 1912.

The American Heritage Picture History of the Civil War. New York: American Heritage Publishing Company, 1960.

Atlas to Accompany the Official Records of the Union and Confederate Armies. 3 vols. Washington, D.C.: U.S. Government Printing Office, 1891-95.

Barrett, John G. *The Civil War in North Carolina.* Chapel Hill: University of North Carolina Press, 1963.

Battles and Leaders of the Civil War. Edited by Robert Underwood Johnson and Clarence Clough Buel. 4 vols. New York: The Century Company, 1884.

Bishop, Jim. *The Day Lincoln Was Shot.* New York: Harper and Row, 1955.

The Blue and the Gray: The Story of the Civil War as Told by Participants. Edited by Henry Steele Commager. Indianapolis: Bobbs-Merrill Company, 1950.

Boatner, Mark Mayo III. *The Civil War Dictionary.* New York: David McKay Company, 1959.

Bruce, Robert V. *Lincoln and the Tools of War.* Indianapolis: Bobbs-Merrill Company, 1956.

Butler, Benjamin F. *Butler's Book.* Boston: A. M. Thayer Company, 1892.

Catton, Bruce. *Mr. Lincoln's Army.* Garden City: Doubleday and Company, 1962.

———. *A Stillness at Appomattox.* Garden City: Doubleday and Company, 1953.

———. *This Hallowed Ground.* Garden City: Doubleday and Company, 1956.

Civil War Naval Chronology, 1861–1865. Compiled by the Naval History Division of the U.S. Navy. Washington, D.C.: U.S. Government Printing Office, 1971.

Clark, Champ. *Decoying the Yanks: Jackson's Valley Campaign.* Chicago: Time-Life Books, 1984.

Cochran, Hamilton. *Blockade Runners of the Confederacy.* Indianapolis: Bobbs-Merrill Company, 1957.

Coggins, Jack. *Arms and Equipment of the Civil War.* Garden City: Doubleday and Company, 1962.

Confederate Receipt Book: A Compilation of Over One Hundred Receipts, Adapted to the Times. Athens: University of Georgia Press, 1980.

Cromie, Alice. *A Tour Guide to the Civil War*. New York: E. P. Dutton and Company, 1975.

Davis, Burke. *Our Incredible Civil War*. New York: Holt, Rinehart and Winston, 1960.

Davis, William C. *Battle at Bull Run: A History of the First Major Campaign of the War*. Baton Rouge: Louisiana State University Press, 1977.

―――. *Duel Between the First Ironclads*. Baton Rouge: Louisiana State University Press, 1975.

Dickey, Thomas, and Peter George. *Field Artillery Projectiles of the American Civil War*. Atlanta: Arsenal Press, 1980.

Dictionary of American Biography. 20 vols. New York: Charles Scribner's Sons, 1940.

The Dictionary of National Biography. 20 vols. London: Oxford University Press, 1917.

Dyer, Frederick H. *A Compendium of the War of the Rebellion*. National Historical Society and Morningside Press, 1979.

Eaton, Clement. *Jefferson Davis*. New York: The Free Press, 1977.

Flood, Charles B. *Lee: The Last Years*. Boston: Houghton Mifflin Company, 1981.

Foote, Shelby. *The Civil War: A Narrative*. 3 vols. New York: Random House, 1954–78.

Fox, William F. *Regimental Losses in the American Civil War, 1861–1865*. Albany: Brandow Printing Company, 1898.

Freeman, Douglas Southall. *Lee's Lieutenants: A Study in Command*. 3 vols. New York: Charles Scribner's Sons, 1942–44.

―――. *R. E. Lee*. 4 vols. New York: Charles Scribner's Sons, 1934–35.

Fuller, Claud E. *Firearms of the Confederacy*. Lawrence: Quarterman Publications, 1944.

Hattaway, Herman, and Archer Jones. *How the North Won: A Military History of the Civil War.* Urbana: University of Illinois Press, 1983.

Horn, Stanley F. *The Army of Tennessee.* Indianapolis: Bobbs-Merrill Company, 1941.

The Image of War: 1861–1865. Edited by William C. Davis. 6 vols. Garden City: Doubleday and Company, 1981–84.

Jones, J. William. *Christ in the Camp: Religion in Lee's Army.* Richmond: B. F. Johnson and Company, 1887.

Jones, Virgil Carrington. *The Civil War at Sea.* 3 vols. New York: Holt, Rinehart, and Winston, 1961.

———. *Ranger Mosby.* Chapel Hill: University of North Carolina Press, 1944.

Kunhardt, Philip B. *A New Birth of Freedom: Lincoln at Gettysburg.* Boston: Little, Brown and Company, 1983.

Leech, Margaret. *Reveille in Washington, 1860–1865.* New York: Harper and Brothers, 1941.

Long, E. B. *The Civil War Day by Day: An Almanac, 1861–1865.* Garden City: Doubleday and Company, 1971.

Lord, Francis A. *Civil War Collector's Encyclopedia.* New York: Stackpole Books, 1963.

Lucas, Marion B. *Sherman and the Burning of Columbia.* College Station: Texas A&M Press, 1976.

McDonough, James Lee. *Shiloh—in Hell Before Night.* Knoxville: University of Tennessee Press, 1977.

———, and Thomas L. Connelly. *Five Tragic Hours: The Battle of Franklin.* Knoxville: University of Tennessee Press, 1980.

McFeely, William S. *Grant: A Biography.* New York: W. W. Norton and Company, 1981.

McPherson, James M. *Ordeal by Fire: The Civil War and Reconstruction*. New York: Alfred A. Knopf, 1982.

McWhiney, Grady, and Perry D. Jamieson. *Attack and Die: Civil War Military Tactics and the Southern Heritage*. University: University Press of Alabama, 1982.

Mitchell, Joseph. *The Badge of Gallantry: Recollections of Civil War Congressional Medal of Honor Winners*. New York: Macmillan Publishing Company, 1968.

Official Records of the Union and Confederate Navies in the War of the Rebellion. 30 vols. Washington, D.C.: U.S. Government Printing Office, 1894–1922.

Photographic History of the Civil War. Edited by Francis Trevelyan Miller. 10 vols. New York: The Review of Reviews Company, 1911.

Randall, James G. *The Civil War and Reconstruction*. Boston: D. C. Heath and Company, 1961.

Roske, Ralph J., and Charles Van Doren. *Lincoln's Commando: The Biography of Commander William B. Cushing, USN*. New York: Harper and Row, 1957.

Scharf, Thomas J. *History of the Confederate States Navy*. New York: Rogers and Sherwood, 1887.

Sears, Stephen W. *Landscape Turned Red: The Battle of Antietam*. New Haven: Ticknor and Fields, 1983.

Smart, Charles. *The Medical and Surgical History of the War of the Rebellion*. Washington, D.C.: U.S. Government Printing Office, 1880.

Soldier Life in the Union and Confederate Armies. Edited by Philip Van Doren Stern. Bloomington: Indiana University Press, 1961.

Stackpole, Edward J. *They Met at Gettysburg*. Harrisburg: Stackpole Books, 1956.

Starr, Louis M. *Bohemian Brigade: Civil War Newsmen in Action.* New York: Alfred A. Knopf, 1954.

Swanberg, W. A. *First Blood: The Story of Fort Sumter.* New York: Charles Scribner's Sons, 1957.

Wakelyn, Jon L. *Biographical Dictionary of the Confederacy.* Westport: Greenwood Press, 1977.

Warner, Ezra J. *Generals in Blue.* Baton Rouge: Louisiana State University Press, 1964.

―――. *Generals in Gray.* Baton Rouge: Louisiana State University Press, 1959.

The War of the Rebellion: A Compilation of the Official Records of the Union and Confederate Armies. 128 vols. Washington, D.C.: U.S. Government Printing Office, 1880–1901.

Watkins, Sam R. *Co. Aytch: A Side Show of the Big Show.* New York: Collier Books, 1962.

Widener, Ralph W., Jr. *Confederate Monuments.* Washington, D.C.: Andromeda Association, 1982.

Wiley, Bell I. *The Life of Billy Yank.* Baton Rouge: Louisiana State University Press, 1952.

―――. *The Life of Johnny Reb.* Baton Rouge: Louisiana State University Press, 1943.

Williams, T. Harry. *The History of American Wars.* New York: Alfred A. Knopf, 1981.

INDEX

191